virtual team excellence

GW00720470

contents

Published by HRCgroup
hrc-group.com

Copyright © 2014 HRCgroup

ISBN 978-0-9929650-0-6

A catalogue record for this book is available from the British Library

Design & layout by Phil Bushell Design & Publishing, London, UK
philbushell@blueyonder.co.uk

Printed & bound by CPI Group (UK) Ltd, Croydon, CR0 4YY

introduction

When we ask managers to identify the most daunting challenge they face on a daily basis, at the top of the list is 'motivating my team'. This is a common theme no matter the nature of the work performed, the business sector, the size of the organisation, the national culture or the number of locations covered. An in-depth examination of this challenge reveals the impact that globalisation, advances in telecommunications and networking technologies, off-shoring, the increasing emphasis on flexible working and work/life balance are having on the way managers approach motivation and team performance. They report an increase in the prevalence of what is often called a 'distributed workforce', or the use of virtual teams, where staff work in remote settings.

Scan your organisation and you will see this trend emerging in the form of working from home policies, dispersed offices, hot-desking in different offices or regions, and the increasing use of virtual project teams working in different locations, regions, countries and continents. These forms of working often require being a member of diverse and multiple delivery teams - virtual teams - to complete the work, and may range from informal, loosely associated teams to classic project delivery teams. Whatever the type of team, this raises a very important set of questions – how do you motivate a virtual team? Is leading and participating as a member of a virtual team different from an intact team? How can you and your organisation encourage people working in virtual teams to work well together across departmental, organisational, cultural and geographic boundaries, to deliver results quickly, effectively, and consistently? Is there a difference between a virtual project and a virtual management team?

What is surprising is the lack of coherent, easy-to-use guidance on best practices to answer these questions about virtual teams. Through our work and experience over twenty-five years with virtual teams across the world, in diverse industries and in multi-national and multi-cultural organisations, we have identified a number of critical factors and behavioural competencies to ensure the success of virtual teams. This book answers your questions about virtual teams by introducing you to the Seven Steps to Virtual Team Excellence and Success. The seven steps provide you with a practical, easy-to-use framework for planning, organising, deploying and assessing virtual teams, and for managing individuals working remotely within these teams. It offers tools to effectively lead virtual teams, the skills and perspectives for successfully participating in virtual teams, and recommendations for managing and fostering the behaviours of high-performing virtual teams. We will introduce you to the Virtual Team Model (VTM), which addresses the behavioural dimensions you will face in developing and managing virtual teams.

Our goal – we want you to develop sustainable best practices that enable your virtual teams to be successful. Chapters one and two examine the challenges and opportunities of virtual working, by addressing the organisational constraints and business imperatives that drive the use of virtual teams. Chapters three to nine, the seven steps – Vision, Involvement, Relationships, Technology, Understanding, Alignment, Let's Go – provide answers to these challenges. Chapter ten looks to the future.

How do you orientate your organisation effectively to support virtual team working as part of the vision and strategy? How do you ensure the involvement of virtual team members in the planning and decision-making of their work? How do you get them to collaborate when distance separates them? How do you build relationships when many differing cultural and emotional dimensions are at play? How do you develop communication and trust? How do you ensure the most appropriate technology is available throughout the organisation? Is it reliable and available to all virtual team members? How do you develop understanding of the challenges and uniqueness of virtual teams? How do you develop culturally fluent managers and stakeholders?

How do you provide virtual teams with structure and support? How does alignment work in practice? Does the organisation's performance management system lend itself to the unique features of virtual teams and take into account managing the members' careers? When you have explored all the above challenges, you will be ready to launch virtual team working. Let's go! But how? How do you select individuals for virtual teams, how do you know they are ready for this type of team working, what will be their roles, what problems may they encounter?

The seven steps of the Virtual Team Model provide you with a roadmap to embrace virtual team working as a business tool. We have been using the seven steps in our client work with virtual teams for over twenty years to provide managers and virtual team members with a comprehensive and practical tool for setting up and managing virtual teams.

Throughout this book we use the term 'virtual team' as this is the term we find organisations use most often. However, the words remote working, teleworking, distributed working, distance working are also used in some organisations. We use the term 'virtual team' to include a broad range of virtual working environments. These may be a staff or project team brought together by a manager or different managers for a unified purpose or project; a task force or business SWOT team organised to deliver a specific set of outcomes; or a series of individual employees coordinating an effort working on a set of action items. We recognise this broad view of virtual teams is open to debate. But in practice, the leaders of these forms of 'virtual' team work confront a set of challenges that we specifically address in this book: physical distance (difference in location and time), psychological distance (emotional connection, autonomy and control) and virtual distance (reporting, function, influence and culture.) The Virtual Team Model provides guidance to manage these challenges. Similarly, to make for easier reading, the word 'manager' is used throughout to include project managers, team leaders, team members, ie anyone involved in leading or participating on a virtual team.

Whatever terminology your organisation prefers to use, this book is a handy guide for you to develop consistently successful virtual teams. In each chapter, you will find a thorough review of each area in the Virtual Team Model supported by examples, tips and techniques, as well as questions for you to consider. Our aim is to provide you with the foundations to define your own best practices to develop and manage virtual teams effectively, which you can apply immediately in your work place. Let's explore together the challenges and benefits of Virtual Team Excellence to enable you to achieve virtual team success.

Acknowledgments

We would like to thank all our clients and colleagues who have accompanied and encouraged us on our journey. We are particularly grateful to the many individuals around the world who have participated in our workshops and inspired us with their experiences and anecdotes.

chapter 1

working together but apart

orienting to virtual team working

"All the world's a stage,
And all the men and women merely players."

Shakespeare

Readiness to embrace virtual teams is not an 'all or nothing' decision. In reality, integrating virtual teams into your organisation will often be an iterative process involving trial and error. It may even feel clumsy and incoherent at times. And rarely do organisations adopt a 'big bang' approach to launching virtual teams. Many are created accidentally in response to a business or customer need. In practice, virtual team working involves meeting a business need where it is identified as the most viable delivery method. Likewise, it may not be a method for delivery that meets all forms of business models or cultures. Some organisations may not be suited for using a virtual team approach to delivery. For instance, *Yahoo* changed direction and brought many of their virtual project teams back in-house. This decision was based, in part, on the value gained from the informal or impromptu 'hallway' discussions, the impact on collaboration, and the view that speed and quality were being compromised. These issues are often cited when we discuss the challenges of working as a virtual team. They will be addressed specifically in chapter four in our discussion of collaboration and virtual team work. Our goal in this chapter is to help you assess if your organisation is ready and able to embrace virtual team work and identify best practices critical to success.

Let us begin by clarifying what we mean by a virtual team. Consider this definition: 'a virtual team consists of members (employees, contract staff and/or support staff) separated by boundaries of time and/or distance, who use technology to conduct interpersonal, social and economic exchanges to deliver business outcomes'. We use the term 'team' rather than group since the success of a team requires its members to have a common vision and purpose, goal and agreed approach to working together, and to hold each other mutually accountable for their performance. A team is pro-active and takes the initiative in developing their working relationships. There are also many individuals who are considered remote workers – they work separately across time, space, and organisational boundaries with links strengthened by webs of communication technology – but may not be assigned to or identify with a specific team. Our focus is on those remote workers who are part of a team that works virtually to achieve agreed and specific team-based performance goals and criteria. This may be a short or long-term delivery team, simple or complex project team, ongoing management team, a customer delivery team or a crisis, emergency or disaster delivery team.

You will notice in the definition above that distance and technology define the critical elements of working as a virtual team. Individuals may be dispersed across different continents, in different countries around the world, or at various locations within a country. They may also be located in different parts of a town or city, or in different parts of the same building, or in separate departments. Some individuals may work from home part of the time or all of the time. In some cases, team members are relatively permanent, but in others, they may change depending on the stage of the project or the nature of the work.

Distance creates a number of challenges for you as a manager or team member. It provides little or no opportunity for face-to-face conversations, may create problems in coordinating the work effort, and lead to a lack of normal social interaction and of a sense of belonging. These issues are not unique to virtual teams but are amplified by distance, by your assumptions about what work is, and the level of commitment that your organisation has made to virtual working. In contrast, distance does allow organisations to bring together talent from across an organisation, to access critical contributors who might not otherwise be able to work together due to time, travel and cost restrictions, and to hire and retain the best people regardless of location.

Technology reduces the perception of physical distance between team members, thus enhancing productivity, and providing them with real-time opportunities to work together and deliver results. However, limitations in availability and use of technology may compromise the viability of virtual teams. And the fast pace of technology advancements may support or diminish the perception of distance between individuals.

Both of these critical elements – distance and technology – will require you to consider the added value of working in a virtual manner. For instance, how prepared is your business unit or organisation to embrace virtual working? What are the assumptions underlying the views of typical managers on the nature and role of virtual teams as a business value proposition? And in what ways do distance and technology influence how we handle performance, accountability and building relationships?

Here are some of the assumptions managers of virtual teams often report as informing their views on working in and managing a virtual team.

- virtual working is a 'cheap and cheerful' alternative to traditional teams or work groups due to leveraging the use of technology
- virtual working can harness organisation talent in multiple locations and streamline performance
- virtual working is more cost effective since technology equals cost savings
- virtual working diminishes the need to address the 'human' dimensions of team development – 'out of sight, out of mind'.

The last assumption is particularly interesting, as the premise driving this assumption is based on two factors – face-time takes time, an ingredient in short supply for many managers, and distance diminishes emotional attachment. The human or behavioural dimension of work takes on a more important role in virtual working. We will explore these issues in later chapters.

Is your organisation ready for virtual team working?

Based on the above assumptions, you will need to assess the readiness of your organisation to implement virtual team working. Four key areas should be assessed for readiness: defining the challenges and opportunities, determining management preparedness for virtual team work, examining the benefits and risks associated with virtual team work, and identifying key behavioural competencies of successful virtual team managers.

1. Defining the challenges and opportunities

It is helpful to consider the unique demands virtual team working places on you as a manager. Virtual team working requires you to strike a delicate balance between a series of interpersonal and individual requirements (or the human side) and the demands of customers and key stakeholders in your organisation. This often necessitates creating a hybrid set of management systems and practices to deliver the work of the virtual team, assess performance and define outcomes. It means living daily with a set of virtual team practices that may not always be purpose-built to support the management practices of your organisation.

We have identified several key reasons organisations give for using virtual teams as a management tool.

- virtual teams are efficient vehicles for leveraging the talents and diversity of perspectives of people across the organisation
- technology diminishes the need to co-locate teams enabling virtual teams to operate 24/7
- virtual teams are cost-effective tools to advance business strategies, in particular in supporting environmental goals to reduce the organisation's carbon footprint, and the cost of office space and travel

- the use of virtual teams for cross-functional projects is one of the most powerful business tools in the global market-place
- virtual teams often require stretching the organisational boundaries and rules for working in order to achieve results
- virtual working enhances work-life balance requirements.

In principle, these may reflect sound business practices in today's business environment yet in fact they challenge traditional views of managing and delivering performance. Consider the manager who takes this view of employee engagement: *"If I don't see them working I assume they are not working."* Does this sound familiar? Or consider the manager who takes the following position: *"If I don't trust a person, I can't trust they are working unless I see them at a desk!"* Whilst organisation practice may support virtual working, our individual assumptions about people, culture and our own values shape commitment to working in a virtual team. Yet the move to working in virtual teams gains momentum yearly as the cost, accessibility, and ease of use make it appear to be a valuable business proposition.

2. Determining management preparedness

The next step is to identify the assumptions informing your view of what constitutes a day of work, the value of work relationships, what demonstrates performance, and how you go about implementing business strategies. The same holds true for the cherished assumptions inherent in your organisation culture and management preferences if virtual working is to offer any return on the investment and meet expectations. To help you, let's look at the differences between traditional management practice and the management of virtual teams. In Figure 1 (overleaf), we capture the differences as identified by managers in a range of organisations in global and national settings.

Notice the change in control, accountability and systems in virtual teams. This requires you to make a brutally honest assessment of how comfortable and ready you and your organisation are to support virtual teams, recognising the inherent conflicts that may be created between these three items. Virtual teams will often diminish your level of control over daily activities, limit your flexibility to manage work flow and may even exacerbate the conflict inherent in your organisation's systems and structures designed to evaluate performance.

Figure 1 Differences between virtual teams and management practice

ORGANISATIONAL CRITERIA	VIRTUAL TEAMS	MANAGEMENT PRACTICE
OBJECTIVES/TASKS	Develop or optimise organisational talent from across the organisation	Work with known products or processes
	Specific, targeted goals linked to business strategies	Multiple objectives and goals
	Time limited, focused, and leveraging the use of technology	Optimise on-going processes
PEOPLE	People with different experiences, competencies and values	People with similar experiences and values
	Temporary team composition based on business need	Plan to optimise resource use over time
SYSTEMS	Systems must be created or modified to integrate work	Systems in place to integrate work
RISKS	Higher uncertainty of outcome, time-lines and deliverables	Higher certainty of outcome, cost, and deliverables
	Disturb status quo	Supports status quo

In practice, virtual teams will challenge the assumptions informing your views on effective management, the influence and reliability of organisation systems to manage the work of virtual teams, the nature of individual and team accountability, and the use of performance management systems. It is worth taking the time up front to directly address the potential impact of each of these assumptions on the team – identify the areas of tension around control, accountability, and systems, and define the areas for agreement needed to drive virtual team success. Is your management team ready to assess the impact on control, accountability and the organisation systems of working virtually? Virtual teams produce better results if their work is integrated into the management practices of your organisation.

3.   Examining the benefits and risks

The benefits and risks of virtual team working for team members, management and your organisation differ somewhat from those of co-located or intact teams. In reviewing the benefits and risks, it is important not to lose sight of the vital connection between risk-taking and performance. To appreciate the benefits and mitigate the risks, we focus on four key areas of management practice – vision/ strategy deployment/goal setting, communication, managing change, sustaining systems and structures – and explore the benefits and risks virtual teams offer organisations.

Vision/strategy deployment/goal setting: the benefits include more challenging and innovative approaches to deployment, leveraging knowledge and assets from across the organisation, and supporting flexibility and agility in utilising and fostering diverse viewpoints. The risks include difficulties in executing multiple, divergent business and customer strategies and goals across cultures and time zones at the same time, choosing the wrong people, technology or strategy, and the pressure of organisational politics, internal competition and time demands. We recommend you consider the following actions in developing your virtual team:

- place the development and execution of the organisation's vision, strategy and goals at the heart of the work of the virtual team
- focus on strategic clarity. This means clarifying the value and significance of the virtual team's work to the larger business, defining clearly team member contributions and participation.
- market the value of virtual team work in your organisation. At the core of managing a change in the views of any management group is an organised marketing effort on behalf of virtual team work.

Communication: the benefits include wider dissemination of ideas and information, speed and flexibility of communicating, enhanced exploration and use of technology and the integration of multiple and diverse points of view. The risks include divided loyalties, an unclear division of roles, tasks and goals, a higher possibility of uncoordinated efforts, and lack of technology and infrastructure to support the work of a virtual team. We suggest the following actions to address these issues:

- initial team planning, goal setting and agreement on performance measures directly with management
- a communications audit to include technology, interpersonal skills and organisation culture
- support team-based decisions on communication strategies and technology requirements.

Managing change: this is the 'holy grail' for the successful manager of virtual teams - the ability to foster support from key stakeholders to embrace virtual teams in the face of resistance to change in systems, structures, assumptions and values. Gaining this support offers enhanced flexibility and speed of communication, quick reaction to customer and market requirements, discussion and identification of blockages and resistance to change, open and transparent working relationships and increased motivation due to buy-in and ownership. The risks include the speed of work overwhelming the organisation and management activity, inconsistent coordination of individual and team actions, less informed decision-making and loss of control of the work flow and outcomes. We recommend you consider these actions in developing your virtual team:

- clearly define and consistently review the virtual team's priorities against the business unit and organisational strategy
- place increased importance on developing decision-making habits as a team that link decisions and activities of the virtual team to the strategic priorities of the organisation
- support an environment where developing and evaluating alternative solutions or options to the actions of the virtual team is the norm
- develop a stakeholder strategy and keep it at the centre of virtual team action planning.

Systems and structures: working as a virtual team will require you and management to confront the paradox of ambiguity and control in your organisational climate. This will mean recognising and accepting the complexity of the environment in which a virtual team works. Likewise the need to have a performance management structure that supports the work of the virtual team is critical to its success and its viability as a business tool. The benefits include the ability to support flexible, responsive and consistently applied actions at all levels where the virtual team interacts, quick and agile release of resources, and formal authority replaced by interpersonal, technical and entrepreneurial competencies. The risks of not addressing the issues include burdening the work of the team with organisational systems and structures not suited to its work, conflict with management over roles, responsibilities and reporting requirements, and managing the political issues of shifting power from management to the virtual team. We suggest you consider the following actions:

- agree roles, responsibilities, decision-making habits for virtual team members
- link team systems and structures to stakeholder requirements
- make review sessions an integral part of all virtual meetings to address ambiguity and confusion around managing stakeholders and clients.

4. Key behavioural competencies

What then, are the key behavioural competencies required by managers and leaders to support stable and productive virtual teams? We have found the following set of competency clusters critical to the success of managing and working as a virtual team.

Interpersonal skills:

- assessing the 'mood' of the team in its work and relationships
- building rapport and relationships quickly and then sustaining them
- asking reflective questions
- listening – spotting underlying meanings and process messages
- testing out meaning by summarising and reflecting
- valuing intuition and the need for psychological connection
- understanding and paying attention to cultural difference
- motivating virtually
- getting things done through influence rather than authority
- developing decision-making habits as a team

Use of technology tools:

- clear, direct and concise messages using a variety of media
- flexibility in uses of different media
- matching message to personal preference
- not overwhelming people with data
- including social content in electronic messages

Outcomes oriented:

- establish clear accountabilities
- agree clear measures and standards of team performance
- focus on outcomes and deliverables rather than activities
- set up agreed monitoring arrangements
- maintain focus on both immediate, urgent and long-term goals

Modelling required behaviours:

- give opportunities to test, make mistakes and learn
- operate away from a command and control leadership style
- stick by word and commitments
- macro rather than micro manage
- demonstrate confidence in others

Collaboration:

- assess suitability for virtual working
- make people feel part of a team
- make yourself available to coach and counsel
- provide clarity over team member roles and interdependencies
- commit to making time for team development
- respond quickly and supportively to crises

Letting the virtual team self manage:

- link what people do to the wider organisation
- network extensively with customers and suppliers
- picture position on the ground
- manage time to maintain and schedule social contact

Adapted from: A Smith & A Sinclair, Roffey Park, 2003

Is your organisation ready to benefit from virtual team work? These four competency areas will help you identify and assess the readiness of your organisation to gain the most from using virtual teams as a business tool. From these four areas it is evident that virtual working provides challenges and opportunities requiring more than organising and deploying team members. A brutally honest assessment of the premises guiding the need for virtual teams, a robust debate over the notions of work, performance and rewards, and an exploration of the demands of distance and technology, are critical to the effectiveness of your staff. We will explore these issues in detail in the following chapters and provide a framework for you to use in virtual team work.

To complete the review of your readiness, it is helpful to identify your own assumptions on these issues. You can usefully ask yourself the following questions:

1. In what way does the traditional notion of team work apply or not apply to virtual teams?

2. What is the level of actual management support and comfort in my organisation for using virtual teams to deliver business results?

3. Do we have a set of performance management tools outside the standard organisation tools that are directed towards ensuring the success of virtual teams?

4. What unique competencies or skills (if any) are required in my organisation to ensure the success of virtual teams?

5. How does my organisation's culture influence the support and use of virtual teams?

By exploring these questions you will gain insight into your views on the role, use and selection of virtual teams as a process for managing business across time zones and remote locations, the role that performance management systems play in supporting or in detracting from working in virtual teams, and the role and value of virtual teams as a viable tool to deliver business performance.

chapter 2

virtual teams as a business & management tool

"If we are to enjoy the efficiencies and other benefits of the virtual organisation, we will have to discover how to run organisations more on trust than on control. Virtuality requires trust to make it work; technology on its own is not enough."

Charles Handy

The most common two questions we are asked when discussing virtual teams are: *"How do we deal with management and business resistance to the changes required to successfully deploy virtual teams?"* and *"What is the added value of virtual teams and can we assess it?"* In financial terms, do virtual teams meet the return on the investment (ROI); and in behavioural terms do virtual teams meet the return on expectations (ROE)?

These questions are based on an assumption that virtual teams are unique or distinctive as a management tool. In practice, they are unique in how they operate and distinctive in how they deliver. For management they are an extension of the tools at the disposal of managers to enhance business performance. They have a role to play as a tool alongside other options for delivering the work. Yet the uniqueness of virtual teams as a business tool may raise any number of potentially difficult organisational issues and management challenges as we noted in the previous chapter. Making explicit the role virtual teams play in contributing to the delivery of business results, as well as the readiness of the organisation to embrace virtual teams as a business and management tool, is essential to embedding virtual team work in the culture of your organisation. Furthermore, an appreciation and understanding of the technical, human and organisational dimensions of virtual teams, and agreement on the added value they bring to the strategic focus of business delivery, are crucial.

Simply put, virtual teams will expose complexities and ambiguities in the work environment for you as a manager. Here are some examples:

- your operating environment will be less structured and less predictable. Virtual teams will bring to the forefront those inconsistencies and paradoxes in deploying business strategies, making explicit situations requiring a resolution between two or more opposing positions or ideas
- potential difficulties may emerge in remote communication, the availability of technology or media to communicate, and challenges in multilingual and multicultural working environments
- the requirements of multiple stakeholders, differences in regional or local business unit strategic priorities and management practices, differences in organisational systems, culture, structures and legal requirements, will require taking a step back to examine the environment in which the team will operate and to consider the implications of different perspectives
- the psychological need to establish human connections: our ability to empathise, our wish to belong and our desire to feel part of a community is often overlooked. Managing this need can be an issue in your virtual teams and remote working environments.

Inevitably, many of these elements will merge and present several potential perspectives. In deploying virtual teams there are few universal rights and wrongs or clear answers to these strategic and psychological dilemmas. And we have found no fool-proof tools for consistent success working across business units, across functions and across cultures.

For these reasons, you may view virtual teams with some scepticism. The primary reason for such reluctance may be due to a lack of conviction that they can deliver results more effectively and efficiently than other methods. You may also be concerned about the requirements for using virtual teams effectively, and the degree of flexibility and risk you are willing to take. Such reluctance is understandable, given the performance demands managers face on a daily basis.

So how do you overcome this reluctance? Working with an unknown or untested management tool such as a virtual team without ample guidance may lead you to not pursue and adopt the tool. When trying to understand new information and ways of working, a change in perspectives, or challenging habits, assumptions and expectations, may be required. Eighty per cent of the challenge in changing your perspective is awareness of its influence on your point of view. The other twenty per cent is challenging the perspective to test if the assumptions informing it are still valid. Critically reflecting on the perspective, including opposing assumptions and evidence to support them, can help you transform your perspective, enabling you to examine your ways of thinking and come up with new or simply different ways of thinking about the way you manage a virtual team.

A few years ago we were working with a regional technology company in the Middle East. Engineers were organised as a virtual project team to deliver a complex project developing a unique, state-of-the-art telecommunications metering system for multiple government clients. Key to the delivery was the use of a high tech production facility, supported by technical experts from business units in other parts of the region. To deliver the project they relied heavily on utilising expertise available only from two countries in the region with competing religious, political, cultural and economic interests. This provoked resistance amongst a small number of the virtual team members leading to these members asking to leave the project or reducing their contribution. The use of a third party as facilitator, case studies, critical incident reports and facilitated discussions with team members provided an opportunity to address directly the implications of working as a virtual team and with members of different backgrounds on this project. The initial work was done using remote technology but the nature of the challenges required meeting face-to-face to resolve the matter. Herein lies the challenge of virtual team work – at times the work of the team may need to be face-to-face to ensure project and team success.

In the previous chapter we noted that overcoming a number of long maintained and cherished assumptions held sacrosanct by management and team members can prove difficult. In the situation above, a small number of team members reported discomfort, fear and emotional turmoil. Most team members found the discussions examining their assumptions uncomfortable yet helpful for revising their ways of thinking about working as a virtual team. At the end of the discussions, three team members chose to be replaced. The project did not deliver the metering system on time but the virtual team is now working on a second project together.

This example provides an insight into the use of critical reflection to transform your perspectives. Most of these virtual team members found the idea of working with members from other countries more anxiety provoking than the actual experience of working together. Challenging taken-for-granted assumptions in culturally appropriate ways is key. In essence, managers and team members are given permission to step beyond the comfort of habits and consider different or new ways of approaching virtual teams.

To help you through this process here is a set of tools that may prove useful to you:

- Critical incident reports examine immediate or past performance against expectations by critically examining the factors helping and hindering the outcome. They provide a tailored, business-specific tool for addressing simple or complex problems faced by virtual teams
- The case study method is an oral or written record of a situation or event examined with the benefit of hindsight. A case study enables you to apply critical thinking and analysis skills to gain new insights and perspectives on events
- Facilitated discussions offer an opportunity to examine performance outcomes against expectations in the company of peers with a mutual interest. They are collaborative in nature and require a degree of personal courage and analytical ability

- **Reflective questioning** is an enquiry into an event designed to test ideas, stimulate thinking, challenge assumptions and clarify understanding. The goal is to arouse interest in an issue by eliciting opinions and feelings, the sharing of relevant experience and interests with answers leading to further questions.

These tools may be supported by a number of your organisational stakeholders – management, peers and supervisors, experienced third parties, an internal or external facilitator or a person who can provide feedback as a direct result of experience participating in or managing the deployment of virtual teams.

Where do we go from here?

We have explored the nature and role of virtual teams as a tool for enhancing business performance, and maintain that managers and members of virtual teams need to reconsider their perspectives on how things get done, challenge their assumptions, often uncritically assimilated, on the nature and role of managing people, and adopt a habit of team-based decision-making. We also maintain that the success of virtual teams rests on members engaging or 'showing up' to embrace the work of the team.

Example: *Word Association* was set up as a marketing and PR agency, with staff in an office in the UK. After a few years growing the business, the owner and MD decided to take a year off and travel in Europe with his young family. He kept in touch with the UK by phone and email so that he could still be involved at a distance. When he returned, he questioned why his employees needed to be in the office at all; if he could run the business from a long way away, why could his people not be located remotely? He closed the office down and everyone started working from home. Ten years later he is running a thriving business with a dozen people working from home: turnover has doubled and staff numbers increased, productivity and staff satisfaction are high. They use instant messaging and the telephone regularly, and hold weekly progress meetings to exchange information.

Adapted from *Future Work* (Maitland and Thomson, 2011)

When formulating and communicating about virtual teams, you will discover opportunities to interpret and define how you think about virtual working and communicate about it to team members. You will be confronted with the assumptions informing how you think about virtual team work leading you to consider taken-for-granted or uncritically assimilated assumptions.

The Virtual Team Model (VTM) offers an effective, yet simple, approach to help you reflect on your assumptions, explore their impact on your expectations of virtual team work and consider new ways of thinking about virtual teams.

This enables the work of the team to have meaning and focus despite distance and time-zone changes. You should also allow team members to express their views on the structures and tools for working as a team and managing their performance, and to have a view of their work and the deliverable within the climate of the business.

In the last two chapters we have discussed the core issues and challenges managers and team members face in leading and managing virtual teams. In the following chapters we share with you the practical value of the VTM, and provide you with the opportunity to explore and develop best practices and key competencies required to achieve sustainable excellence and success in virtual team working.

Figure 2 Virtual Team Model (VTM)

© Shawn Ireland 2012

THE WIS STORY – PART ONE

Let us introduce you to Wex International Systems (WIS), a global organisation with offices in Europe, Africa, Asia, the Middle East, North and South America. At the end of each of the following chapters, we follow WIS on their journey to virtual team excellence and success using the Virtual Team Model.

As part of their strategy to improve efficiency and performance across the organisation, they decided to develop a global knowledge management database (KSI). This would provide up-to-date information online to all their offices world-wide, enabling all regions to share information and experiences in a timely fashion.

The KSI project was critical for WIS, as it was a major global project, bringing together team members from across the world – the first major virtual team project they had implemented, and of strategic importance. There was a substantial budget of some $3 million, with a pilot system to be tested within 12 months. A further significant budget was available for the launch and roll-out within 18 months.

The project sponsor, together with key stakeholders around the world and within the organisation, recruited employees to the virtual project team. They represented the various business interests across the organisation and from each region. Virtual team working was key to the success of the KSI project.

case study the WIS story

chapter 3

vision

"Clarity affords focus."

Thomas Leonard, coach & mentor

When people work as members of virtual teams it is sometimes difficult to appreciate how these types of teams fit within the organisation's strategy, as their purpose seems unclear. Distance between people, the type of work, workplace norms, types of working relationships, the level of trust, all may conspire to erode the continuity and clarity of individual or virtual team working. And despite the best efforts of yourself, as a manager, to provide structure and consistency, the fact of managing from a distance and organisation politics may exacerbate the situation.

A vision, supported by strategic clarity, will help you align the work of individuals and your teams with the organisation's stated and implied vision. It links the role and goals of virtual team work to the strategic goals of the organisation, whether they are clear or ambiguous in nature.

During a session with senior managers of an international organisation, we asked them to draw a picture of their experience of how it felt to be working in the company at present. One team produced a blank piece of paper and scribbled all over it. They explained that they were experiencing chaos as it felt as if they were working in a vacuum. What they needed was a clear sense of direction, a compass bearing like magnetic north, to focus their energies on a vision and strategy.

In its basic form, strategic clarity diminishes this vacuum by linking the existence of virtual team work to the overall vision and strategic intent of the business. It is critical then for virtual team members to have a more expansive view on how the significance of the work of the virtual team fits into the overall organisation vision, and to show their commitment, since:

- working virtually often fosters independent actions and decisions outside the traditional organisation structures
- teams have to operate and think more strategically especially in response to the immediate needs for action
- the more urgent and meaningful the outputs of the individual and team, the more management will need to link the work of the virtual team to the overall focus and direction of the business
- the need to negotiate a set of clearly defined, relevant and targeted performance goals within the strategy is directly linked to the success of virtual team performance.

A co-funded regional development project in Eastern Europe supported by the European Union and the United States Agency for International Development (USAID) required a virtual team to deploy a development project from five capital cities. The delivery of the project was critical to establishing key targets for the redevelopment of the region. Due to the political, cultural and linguistic dimensions of the project, the team members initiated the project by meeting in person as a team prior to the launch. Following the meeting, team representatives met with key stakeholders from the organisations involved, with the specific goal of understanding how the project fitted into the mandate and overall strategy of their respective organisations. The team defined the vision and supporting strategic goals, planning and delivery strategies, as well as their performance criteria to reflect the purpose and intent of the sponsoring organisations. They also developed a narrative to share these with their stakeholders. These activities were particularly difficult as the team had to overcome conflicting goals, diverse expectations, cultural ambiguities, and political/economic strategies influencing the sponsoring organisations and the receiving agencies.

A project post-mortem conducted at the close of the project was revealing. Creating a narrative that framed the context of the project, including its vision, strategy and goals around the goals of the sponsoring organisations significantly modified the working structure, planning and implementation of the project, informed the types of technology used to communicate, shifted the choice of location, language and delivery methods, and required virtual team members to negotiate local arrangements for project support and materials. It also informed the choice of evaluation criteria chosen by the virtual team to judge their performance.

To support the development of a vision, you are encouraged to address the following issues at the beginning of the virtual team's life – to create a 'team charter'. The orientation process requires you to take a view on the following key questions:

1. What are the expectations of the organisation for promoting virtual team work for this deliverable? Is a virtual team the most potent way of delivering the project or outcomes? On the surface this would appear self-evident as a leader or member of a virtual team. A brutally honest discussion with key stakeholders of expectations will foster transparency and trust – critical ingredients to success.

2. What are the specific deliverables expected from this approach to working and how do they fit with the vision and strategy of the business unit or organisation? This may or may not be understood or specified. On a project virtual team this is an integral part of the initial planning process. Simple, unambiguous, clearly worded definitions and descriptions of the deliverables are critical to foster team cohesion.

3. What gaps exist between the strategic intent of your team and the larger organisation strategy that impact your ability to work together and/or achieve your goals? Using simple language and

appropriate business terminology, identify any inconsistencies inherent in your virtual team's strategy and the larger strategic intent of the organisation. In our experience, gaps between the team and organisation strategies foster inconsistent decision making and actions among team members.

4. Has a stakeholder analysis been conducted to identify stakeholders crucial to the success of this form of working? What are their positions (opposed, neutral, supportive), and what stakeholder strategies will be deployed to assist their working relationships? Post-mortems of dysfunctional virtual teams yield rich sources of recommendations for action. A key finding is the necessity of a timely and supported stakeholder analysis. In our work, consistently successful virtual teams have leaders that support the development and on-going review and revision of a stakeholder management action plan. Complexity or simplicity are not as critical to success as consistent and timely review.

5. What are the organisational and political constraints to achieving the deliverables successfully? This question is often answered using stakeholder analysis.

6. To be successful, what organisational practices must change, what must stop, what must be modified, and what must be created? These questions speak for themselves. The answers require the team to explore what organisational practices work and do not work to make the team successful.

7. Do you have a narrative or story to tell about your team? Most people love a good story. Humans use story-telling to communicate the essence of an idea, describe experience, sell an idea or value. Consistently successful virtual team leaders sell their team and its work by sharing the team's story and developing a narrative around that story. It communicates the essence of the team's vision for their work to the rest of the organisation and key stakeholders.

These questions are broad and holistic in nature placing the team at the heart of the project or deliverable. The deployment of virtual teams, therefore, requires a more complete view of the strategic intent of the business in order to understand the goals as they relate to the mandate of virtual teams.

How do we implement the vision?

At the inception of virtual teams, you are encouraged to agree protocols for the following:

- to link the role of the virtual team deliverable directly to the vision and strategic intent of the business unit and/or organisation. Clearly define the virtual team vision and strategy in simple terms
- to address divergent or conflicting business unit goals/expectations within the peer group of remote individuals and/or the virtual team, and with the manager
- to market, sell and place the work of the virtual team work within the broader context of the organisation
- to manage expectations of management over control, accountability, performance, managing stakeholders and deliverables
- to sustain the motivation and momentum of the work over time.

QUESTIONS FOR YOU TO CONSIDER

1. Can the virtual team vision and strategy be stated in simple, straightforward and unambiguous language?

2. What are the gaps (if any) in the virtual team's vision and strategy and that of the organisation? How will these gaps be managed?

3. How tolerant is management to individuals working virtually in teams acting 'independently' yet within the confines of the overall strategic intent of the organisation?

4. Will management feel confident supporting actions that do not sit within the traditional decision-making structures of the organisation?

5. Are you able to clearly define 'magnetic north' (focus on the general direction) for your virtual team?

6. Have you developed a compelling narrative or story-line that is meaningful and relevant to sell the vision of the team and support its 'magnetic north'?

THE WIS STORY – PART TWO

To set the project up for a flying start, the project sponsor brought the key stakeholders and all virtual team members together for a face-to-face meeting so that they could get to know each other, understand their respective roles and responsibilities and areas of expertise. The purpose of the meeting was also to explain fully the KSI project and answer any questions or queries.

The project sponsor spelled out the critical nature of the KSI project to WIS, and the reasons to utilise a global virtual team. The overall vision and strategy of the organisation were explained clearly, and how the aims of the KSI project fitted in with this strategy. The project was certainly challenging but would reap excellent benefits once the knowledge management database was up-and-running. Discussions ensued with the key stakeholders to clarify their understanding of the project. The team manager and members of the virtual team agreed how they would work together over the coming months to develop the project plan. This would include the project deliverables/goals, the team's strategy, and a comprehensive stakeholder analysis. They would also review the organisation's processes, systems and technologies to recommend changes that would help them achieve the project successfully and in a timely fashion. Innovative ways to keep team members motivated would also be examined.

case study the WIS story

chapter 4

involvement

*"Coming together is a beginning,
keeping together is progress,
working together is success."*

Henry Ford

This quote by Henry Ford offers a simple definition of our view of involvement in team work and is relevant to virtual teams. Involvement is more than just going through the motions of working on a virtual team – it is consciously making an intellectual and emotional investment in the relationships and outputs of the virtual team. What makes involvement challenging for virtual team members is balancing three psychological demands that influence a person's approach to team work: autonomy, control and collaboration. The behavioural sciences provide a diverse source of research and writing that define and operationalise each of these three demands.

In virtual team work, we define autonomy, control and collaboration in specific terms based on the research and writing in the field of social psychology and group dynamics, which provide relevant linkages to the unique psychological requirements of virtual working.

Let us explore the role of Involvement in the work of your virtual team:

Figure 3 **The teamwork triangle**

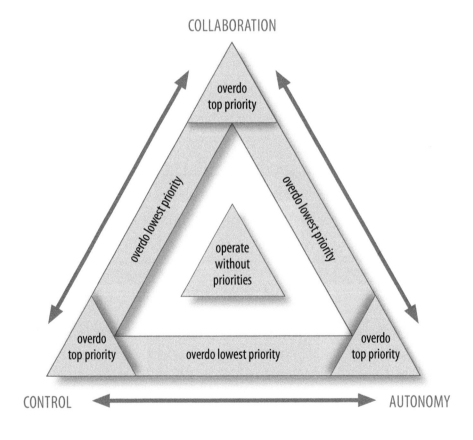

Adapted from *Three Types of Teamwork*, SMG

What does *autonomy* look like?

Virtual teams must accomplish work that is often complex, non-routine, delegated, and may or may not be determined in advance. For non-routine tasks, your team may be required to take independent decisions using their own judgment in the absence of immediate face-to-face contact or access to you via technology. This creates ambiguity and a lack of clarity which is uncomfortable, even scary, for some team members, yet a motivator for others depending on their personal psychological requirement for flexibility or structure. Consider how you would feel taking a quick decision on a budget without feedback or data. This may be easy for you yet scary to others without more detail and support.

For delegated tasks, your team may be required to deliver specific outcomes, with the activity and outcomes pre-determined. Consider how you might react to a project plan with little or no flexibility in deliverables. This might be frustrating for you but offer security and comfort for others who require the structure. In both cases, as a manager you are confronted with four key questions:

1. What work needs to be delegated and what are the non-routine work deliverables for your virtual team?

2. What is the tolerance of my virtual team members to routine and non-routine work?

3. Where is the right balance of routine and non-routine work for the given needs of the virtual team members?

4. How engaged is the team with the goals and demands of their work?

To address autonomy as a manager, we suggest you get to know the tolerance for ambiguity as well as structure in your team members. If they handle autonomy well, be sure to take a hands–off approach to these people, set individual goals in consultation with all team members, agree resources and then get out of the way of these individuals. If they do not handle autonomy well and require more structure, set individual and team goals and organise consistent and timely 'stealth' sessions via an agreed technology platform to review the work and results. Stealth sessions are brief, highly focused, meetings planned in advance. They last no more than ten minutes and focus on the most critical issues facing the team member. If you are a member of the virtual team, agree with other team members your requirements for autonomy and/or structure. Agree to be more assertive when structure is not sufficient or too cumbersome and be sure to support this type of interaction among team members.

What does *control* look like?

A virtual team is a social environment which creates unique and distinctive interactions requiring each team member to adjust or regulate their behaviour. This actively determines the level of involvement in the work of the team. You may be familiar with the tension of working to a plan or strategy as a virtual team. Some members are rigorous in following the plan whilst others seem to ignore it or find the plan cumbersome or annoying. In line with autonomy, control reflects the individual and social needs of virtual team members to regulate and adjust their behaviour to meet the demands of the team tasks.

For instance, a team member may place a high value on detail, organisation and predictability, with success measured in how well this is executed. Another team member may place a high value on flexibility, spontaneity and the freedom to go where the mood takes them. Each style requires regulating and adjusting to meet the mutual requirements of the team. This recognises the need in business for predictability, reliability and consistency, yet faces the real challenge of virtual team work – the potential loss of direct management control. This can be unsettling for many managers prompting a high degree of structure for a virtual team. A balanced approach to managing individual control leads to virtual team success.

To address control as a manager, we suggest recognising the tension between the need for control and the potential loss of direct control inherent in virtual team work. Accept the possible futility of expecting on-site control of virtual teams. Acknowledge the value of a balanced approach, working with your team to agree a level of systems and structures commensurate with the goals of the team. This requires taking a hands-on approach with team members, discussing individual and team requirements, establishing decision-making routines or 'habits' for working, and setting individual and team goals unilaterally. Maximise the opportunity to develop new habits by working with the team to establish and agree an action plan, laying out incremental pathways for the team deliverable via detailed plans, and support their comments and contributions to the plan. Control does not mean leading or being authoritarian but rather the psychological need of virtual team members for predictability, reliability and consistency of the plan the team follows and the goals and objectives that are agreed and delivered.

How do we maximise the development of virtual team routines or habits? Charles Duhigg, in his book *The Power of Habit* (2012) notes that people and groups have 'keystone' habits, that do not rely on getting actions and decisions right all of the time, but on identifying a few key priorities, agreeing cues for acting on these priorities and then fashioning them into key drivers for the virtual team. Keystone habits are agreed by the team, practised and reviewed, and rewarded when performed. These keystone habits provide control in a virtual environment, whilst balancing the flexibility of a virtual environment. Your action plan will identify habits, some possibly new, to shape how members manage control.

What does *collaboration* look like?

In its basic form, collaboration on a team is greater than the contribution of a single member. Collaboration is working jointly with others on a level playing field. In our work with virtual teams, we have found collaboration is more attractive than competition amongst team members. Trust, camaraderie, and sharing expertise willingly demonstrates collaboration. Team members are more inclined to work together, especially when time and distance are factors in the work of the team.

Consider the following example. In a motor racing team, one member will win the race while other members lose. However, motor racing also has a collaborative dimension to it. The racing 'team' can only achieve its goal of winning if the team members work as a unit. Only by collaborating in their efforts, and with a focus on the outcome, will they be successful.

We are often asked what impact distance and the use of technology have on the spontaneity and impromptu interactions in face-to-face teams. Technology and social media will foster collaboration if you can find common ground in their choice – wikis, blogs, online forums and collaboration tools – for problem-solving, sharing best practices and managing team issues and expectations. The chip maker *Xilinx* reported an increase in productivity of 25% using diverse social media to tackle strategic and client issues. They can foster the spontaneous, impromptu interactions consistent with face-to-face collaboration.

To address collaboration as a manager, do not be afraid of social media as a collaboration tool. Train team members to be collaborative – it may not be comfortable or feel natural for some virtual team members. Work together with your virtual team to establish a simple, clear strategy linked to SMART goals, and help them collaborate to achieve the goals, intervening only when necessary. Support and maximise team-based work in this process. Ensure team roles are clear and understood. In our work we have found collaboration works when members have clearly defined roles in line with the goals of the team. Indeed, collaboration can even work if roles are defined but the team goal is not necessarily clearly defined.

As a virtual team member, commit yourself to build relationships by interacting more with team members via technology including social media, support cross-functional working and increase interactions with all stakeholders that impact the work of the virtual team. Recognise the diverse needs of team members for autonomy and control and value these needs as part of the relationship building process on the virtual team.

A number of collaboration technologies are available to support real-time virtual collaboration. Each month, new apps for phones provide landscapes for specific types of on-line or cloud collaboration, video conference, and desk-top visualisation. We will explore these technologies in Chapter Six. The most potent collaboration tool is face-to-face when a virtual team commences.

Let us return to the triangle. Based on these influencers – autonomy, control and collaboration – where do you think your team is within the triangle? On the following figure, plot your perception of where your team currently falls within the triangle by writing A for actual in one of the eight sections of the triangle. Then write D for desired.

Figure 4 The teamwork triangle

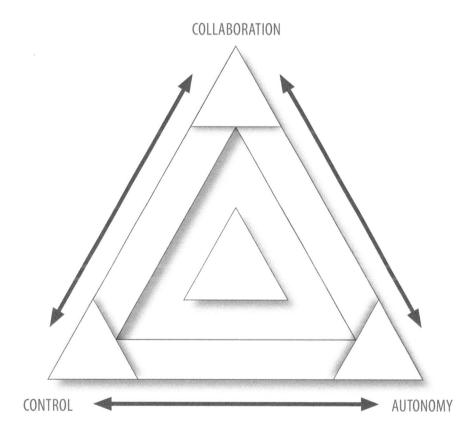

To help you with your team profile, here are a few questions for you to consider:

	A	B	C
1. Which represents your virtual team's most important strategic practice?	Adding value through star performers	Reducing complexity through organisation-wide coordination	Combining resources in novel ways to create innovative solutions
2. How does your virtual team develop expertise?	Hire from outside	Promote from within	Strategic alliances/ partnerships
3. What criterion is most important when evaluating performance?	Individual competence	Formal structure	Working well within a group
4. Who is responsible/ accountable for performance?	Individual	Management	Team
5. What behaviours does the manager/team leader encourage?	Risk taking	Protection against failure	Innovating with existing systems
6. What method does management use to address a problem?	Compartmentalisation of the problem to a discrete area	Mandating the solution	Group process
7. What is the manager's operating style?	Hands-off	Hands-on	Hand-in-hand
8. On what is the service your virtual team provides based?	The individual	The system	The team
9. On what should each virtual team member be focused?	Their own piece of work	Keeping in mind the big picture	Fitting in with what others are doing
10. What purpose do your meetings serve?	As a forum for people to present their views	As a decision-making session	As team-building exercises
11. How does your virtual team expect you to act?	Self-reliant	Compliant	Collaborative
12. What methods are used most to encourage compliance within your virtual team?	Rewards	Rules	Shared values
13. Which of these skills is indispensable in order to be promoted within your team?	Intellectual skills	Political skills	Social skills
14. In general, what motivates most of the members of your virtual team?	Achievement	Power/protection	Affiliation

Count the number of answers you chose for each column and write the totals in the corresponding boxes below.

	A	B	C

AUTONOMY   CONTROL   COLLABORATION

The relative distribution between the three influencers should give you a rough idea of the location of your virtual team on the triangle. The highest number is your current top priority, the middle your second priority, and the lowest is your last priority.

Although all three behavioural influencers – autonomy, control and collaboration – are important to effective virtual team working, our experience shows that collaboration is the most valuable in ensuring a committed and high performing virtual team.

How do I translate these behavioural influencers into action?

Consistently high performing virtual teams demonstrate several common characteristics which shape the expression of the behavioural influencers: a clear, simple vision and strategy with supporting goals and objectives, an understanding of interdependence, cohesiveness, trust, and enthusiasm and workload management. Let's explore each characteristic.

A clear, simple vision and strategy with supporting goals. The strategy and goals are more than a simple understanding of the immediate task; they are rather an overall understanding of the team's vision for a deliverable, its role, its responsibilities, and the things required to achieve the vision. In basic terms, what is the 'magnetic north' for your team and what is the detailed plan for getting there? Vision drives commitment to a strategy and goals, involving all virtual team members in developing the roadmap, defining the goals and relating them to specific activities performed by team members. The time spent on these actions at the beginning of the virtual team's work results in less time needed later to resolve problems and misunderstandings in failing to take these steps. Virtual team development and team efficiency and effectiveness can be maximised by an explicit effort to clarify the vision, strategy, roles, decisions and responsibilities.

Interdependence is the degree to which joint actions are required by virtual team members in order to complete an assignment. Once your virtual team's strategy and goals have been determined, the interdependence of the activities must be consistently supported and encouraged. If everyone does their own thing without a balance between control, autonomy and collaboration, no real virtual team exists. You have a few options to support interdependence. If you are leading a project team, the project plan and corresponding integration technology will make interdependence explicit. A discussion of the expectations of this plan along with a review of the consequences of lack of interdependent working is essential. If the team is less formal in its structure, being explicit at the beginning of the team's work about the assumptions members may have, is helpful. Revisit the reflective questions identified in Chapter Two.

As a virtual team, it is vital to explore the assumptions we bring to the table to define our success and failure as a team. Be specific, focused and intentional in debating this question. Reconsider the assumptions by considering the opposite assumption. For instance, if your team identifies the following assumption – *"we will only get marginal or nominal support for our work by management"* – the opposite assumption is *"we will get the full support of management for this project."* Follow up with this question: *What evidence or data do you have to support the opposite assumptions?* This is a compelling question for it asks the team to consider information outside the comfort zone of the team. Examining and openly discussing the impact of the assumptions members bring to the team, heightens the team's awareness and sensitivity to this issue.

Cohesiveness is the strength of desire all members have to remain as a virtual team and depends on the personal needs that each member can satisfy by belonging to the team. This involves team members discussing their views on working as a virtual team, their values and self-interests.

Cohesiveness increases as the team's ability to meet individual needs increases. Therefore, as a virtual team develops, you, as the manager, need to ensure that individual needs are being met to the highest degree possible.

Trust reflects the virtual team's ability to bring to the surface differences in values and opinions, and to deal with them accordingly. In any team situation, disagreement is likely to occur. The ability to openly recognise conflict and to seek to resolve it through discussion remains critical to a virtual team's success. People do not automatically work well together just because they belong to the same organisation or share the same job function. In order to build working relationships that are characterised by openness and trust, your virtual team must deal with the personal issues arising from working virtually. Creating a sense of mutual trust, respect and understanding and dealing with the inevitable conflicts that occur in any virtual situation are key factors in developing an effective virtual team.

Enthusiasm and workload management are the collective belief that the virtual team can achieve the goal and that members have the capacity to deliver. They are the spirit that affects virtual team members when they begin to believe that they can achieve the goal they have set out to accomplish. To increase the level of vitality it is important for you to reward the early successes of the virtual team. When enthusiasm is manifest, people are more likely to be truly engaged and put in the extra effort necessary to achieve the team goal.

"Human beings have an innate drive to be autonomous, self-determined, and connected to one another. And when that drive is liberated, people achieve more and live richer lives."

Daniel Pink, Drive, 2010

At this point, you may be asking, *"This is fine from a theoretical perspective, but how do I make it come alive for my virtual team?"*

All virtual teams embark on a journey through a series of predictable phases in their work. Each phase meets a specific set of individual and team oriented behavioural requirements, as outlined earlier.

The following development model created by George Buzaglo offers three simple, useful phases for linking virtual team theory and practice. Virtual teams journey through three phases in their work – invite, invest, invent. The role of the leader supports the work of the team in each phase.

Figure 5 **Phases of virtual team working**

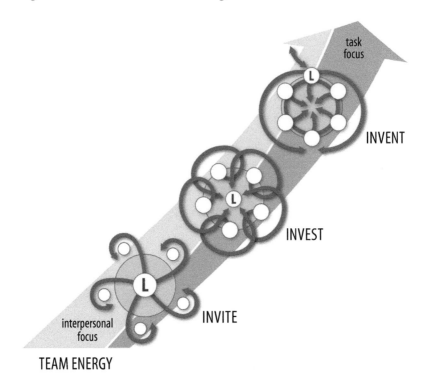

Source: SMG 2000 (Buzaglo)

Structure and behaviour are the core diagnostic criteria for assessing your virtual team's phase in the model.

Let us consider the following diagnostic questions for structure:

STRUCTURE

INVITE PHASE

Do members understand the vision and strategy?

Is alignment needed between virtual team members' interests, skills, the task, wider organisational responsibilities, and their responsibilities to the team?

Are members confused about roles? Do they feel the need to do all tasks together?

Are members reluctant to express opinions openly?

Are the leader's decisions or members' opinions challenged? Are members reluctant to make decisions? Is there difficulty translating decisions into action?

INVEST PHASE

Do members express support for the vision and strategy? Do they shape it in terms of their own personal and role perspective ?

Is alignment needed among roles of members (including the leader) within the virtual team, given the needs of the task?

Although members are negotiating and contesting roles and responsibilities as they relate to the task, is the focus primarily interpersonal?

Does communication break down as roles conflict?

Are members reluctant to compromise? Does the interpersonal focus interfere with skilful decision-making?

INVENT PHASE

Do virtual team members understand and continue to refine the vision and strategy?

Is there a need to focus primarily on the alignment between the virtual team and the organisation?

Are members' roles and responsibilities clear and directly related to the needs of the task?

Is communication very open and effective?

Are members effective decision-makers, flexible, and do they use the needs of the task as criteria to make decisions?

Equally, the behaviours expressed by virtual team members are an important consideration as the virtual team matures through each phase.

Let us reflect on the following diagnostic questions for behaviour:

BEHAVIOUR

INVITE PHASE

Do members do little work without the leader's clear direction?

Are members undecided about their commitment to the virtual team?

Do members trust each other and the team leader?

Are members afraid to take risks?

Do members focus primarily on the leader?

Are members showing signs of anxiety and/or complacency?

The fit between the virtual team structure and task is low. Unless the leader provides structure, it does not exist

INVEST PHASE

Do members do some work independently, so the team is not fully effective?

Are members committed to their individual success on the team but not yet to the virtual team's success?

Has trust increased as roles are better defined?

Are members increasing their own risk-taking?

Do members focus primarily on the team, and on the leader as part of the virtual team?

Are there signs of frustration and unresolved personal conflict?

There is medium and increasing fit between the virtual team structure and the task

INVENT PHASE

Do members reach optimal performance as a virtual team?

Are members committed to both individual and virtual team success?

Do members trust each other?

Are members willing to take significant risks?

Are members focused on the task?

Is enthusiasm prevalent, or is stagnation creeping in?

There is a good fit between the developed structure and the task. In high performance virtual teams, the structure shifts as the task evolves

As your virtual team evolves and becomes established you will want to vary your style of leadership, whether as a manager or team leader.

"You have to be more focused on outcomes, better at communication, more explicit about your expectations, more regular about checking that work is going the right way. You might have to schedule short but more frequent calls to chat with somebody working for you in another place."

A Gregory, IBM Global Business Services, 2009. Equality & Human Rights Commission

The main issue during the invite phase is the commitment of team members. Do they really want to be part of the virtual team? You will be more directive during this phase, giving explicit direction on specific tasks and how these tasks should be accomplished, providing high levels of structure to the virtual team's work. This style is often misinterpreted as highly controlling or hierarchical. Its function is not to dominate, but rather to give direction – pointing the way to the team's end goal. This style helps to provide the initial structure team members need to mature as a virtual team and to direct their attention to the task.

During the invest phase you are building the trust of team members with each other and with yourself. You will be more facilitative, leading team members to begin developing their own structures, monitoring the team to see where stronger, more directive leadership is needed, and providing it when necessary. This style is more 'chameleon-like,' vacillating between being directive when the virtual team needs structure, and empowering to encourage team members to develop their own working structures.

When the team approaches the invent phase, the performance of members is key. Are they really being productive or losing energy and showing a certain inertia? You will need to collaborate with your virtual team members, aiding them in adapting their working structures when necessary and requested. This style is based on the team's maturity and sophistication in adjusting work structures to fit the needs of the task. It emphasises that the virtual team is leading the work and that the team leader is working within the group.

Therefore, to link theory with practice, the following actions are required:

In the invite phase

- provide a simple statement of an initial vision, strategy and goals for the team. Whilst this may be revised later, it provides an initial sense of direction and focus
- give clear and detailed explanations of tasks; break them down into small, manageable components
- use team meetings to answer members' questions about the work with the whole team
- give frequent status reports to show progress and task completion
- identify in detail team members' potential contributions to the team
- clarify the value of the project to the larger organisation
- spell out criteria for participating on the virtual team
- communicate the team's work to the organisation and stakeholders
- define the team members' roles and ensure that all team members understand the roles of others on the team
- establish clear ground rules for the virtual team
- elicit discussion and honest opinions about the project and keep discussion focused on the agenda and task
- encourage participative planning, goal setting, and decision-making.

As the virtual team gets into its stride – the invest phase

- revisit, update and revise the vision, strategy and goals for the team
- reframe interpersonal conflict into task conflict
- ensure that the tasks to be accomplished are clear to team members
- build trust and increase communication among virtual team members
- use the virtual team's goal/the organisation's vision and strategy to make decisions about how to proceed with the project
- maintain role boundaries
- help the virtual team use the natural conflict of this stage as an opportunity for open communication
- help set, model and maintain standards for appropriate team behaviours
- encourage the virtual team to make decisions, but if it cannot, use tactics to facilitate the decision making process.

Once the virtual team is working well – the invent phase

- identify ongoing challenges and pitfalls – strategise with the virtual team about how to solve them
- determine with the team when the task /project is complete
- continue to manage the external organisation's demands on the virtual team
- maintain and provide needed resources to the team
- communicate virtual team learning to the larger organisation
- keep the organisation apprised of the virtual team's progress and continue to gather and share feedback
- encourage mutual interdependence with, and among, virtual team members
- redefine roles and responsibilities as tasks change or become more complex
- challenge 'group-think'
- allow the virtual team to make critical decisions related to the team's goal.

Remember that once your virtual team has achieved its goal, this should be celebrated, and a post-mortem conducted to elicit lessons learned. This is often referred to as the 'mourning process'.

How do we implement Involvement?

At the inception of virtual teams, you are encouraged to agree protocols for the following:

- to agree if a virtual team is the type of team required
- to support the steps to reach *Invent*
- to maintain clear goals in line with the strategy
- to encourage interdependence
- to manage individual needs, sense of achievement and workload of the team
- to agree 'keystone habits'.

QUESTIONS FOR YOU TO CONSIDER

1. What criteria do you take into account when deciding on using a virtual team?

2. What are the key issues in each stage of team development?

3. What is your strategy for managing, autonomy, control and collaboration?

4. How do you build and develop your virtual teams?

5. How do you manage the needs of individual team members and oversee the workload of virtual teams to achieve the goal?

THE WIS STORY – PART THREE

The team manager was adamant that the participation of each team member was paramount for the success of the KSI project. By making the most of each individual's skills and experience, and involving each team member from the outset in the planning phase, the project should progress fairly smoothly. It was a testing time for the team manager, dealing with the varied dynamics of the group. Balancing the needs for autonomy and/or control, together with the need for a collaborative approach was a challenge. Videoconference meetings were held weekly to help develop the team dynamics and understand different personality and behavioural issues. The team manager included various team building activities during these meetings. He drew on his past experiences of managing a group, and varied his leadership approach to suit the situation, starting out as quite directive, detailed and hands-on until he felt individuals had really gelled as a team, when he could operate more 'hands-off'.

The virtual team members were keen to be involved and enthusiastically developed a team charter, their strategy and goals. After reviewing their various areas of expertise and experience, the team also agreed their respective roles and responsibilities. These were exciting times. It was a steep learning curve for all, given that they came from several different cultural backgrounds, and that they had not worked together before. Mutual trust had to be developed and their relationships developed.

case study

the WIS story

chapter 5

relationships

"Understanding human needs is half the job of meeting them."

Adlai Stevenson

I n practical terms, virtual teams are a laboratory for exploring the challenges of relationships. Each team member brings to virtual team working a range of psychological requirements – implicit and explicit needs, goals and expectations – that dictate their level of involvement and commitment to the work. Motivation is directly linked to the level of participation in a team especially around problem-solving, decision-making and resolving the business issues associated with the mandate of the team.

In our work with virtual teams, we have learned a number of key lessons for managing their behaviour. You should be specific and provide details, spell out everything and assume nothing. It is paramount to develop a stakeholder analysis and sustain it at the heart of the team. Do not expect perfection. Remember that virtual team working is different from traditional working environments. And, however good a team manager you may be, this does not necessarily make you a good virtual team manager.

There are four critical psychological dimensions that you need to address: comfort, communication, trust, and relationship building.

Comfort: a direct link exists between the performance of virtual team members and their psychological comfort. They may need to contribute a higher level of emotional energy or secure an 'emotional investment' to achieve success. They may provide differing levels of emotional commitment – the level of emotional investment – to the task. This appears to have no correlation to culture or business environment, but is linked directly to individual psychological needs in response to the ambiguities and clarity of the team's mandate.

Communication: the level of communication (number of times some level of contact and interaction occurs) has a direct impact on the mood and ultimate on-going success of virtual teams. The most successful virtual teams make the effort to meet face-to-face on a consistent basis. A kick-off /orientation meeting, face-to-face, is a good way to promote social interaction, establish common understanding and relationship building in a team. Such a meeting enables team members to acknowledge the purpose of the team and its significance for the organisation, and develop mutual understanding and interdependence. Communication ground rules and expectations should be established, as well as the type of technology deployed by the organisation for virtual teams, the frequency and length of communication, and the format and frequency of interactions. The more focused the discussion, the more effective the deliverables will be.

In any organisation, an environment that fosters mutual respect, creativity, positive interpersonal relations and team working, depends largely upon both the quality of information shared among team members and the efficacy of the communication between them – the mood this fosters amongst team members. Providing network etiquette (or 'netiquette') guidelines is an important component for effective virtual team management. If you establish and implement 'netiquette' standards, you will find it easier to manage and maintain the efficiency and stability of your virtual teams. Consistently supporting these standards will help you and your team maintain and ensure, professionalism, courtesy, and ethical behaviour, and equip team members to avoid informational nuances that may be misinterpreted so easily. You may also lessen the 'communication gap' that is prevalent in virtual communication technologies (ie absence of body language, tone of voice, emotion, and personal interplay).

We should all be sensitive to the difficulties faced in communicating remotely. Here are four peculiarities in virtual communication that we have identified:

- words are imprecise tools for communication. Often we find the ideas we wish to express do not fit easily into words and sentences. This is especially common when communicating across languages – we are unable to say in precise terms what we mean. Remote communication, unlike face-to-face communication, relies heavily on the content of messages to convey meaning. It is therefore essential for virtual team members to take a few moments to reflect back to the others the understanding of words, especially when they may lack clarity, are ambiguous or based on jargon. Be careful not to try to be funny or sarcastic as such messages can be interpreted as just mean or angry.

- distractions interrupt the attention and focus of virtual team members. Depending on the location and use of technology, the emotional state of a team member, the time of day or the level of stress, individuals can be deflected easily from concentrating on the work of the team. The outcome, depending on the mode of communication, is that other things in the immediate environment or within ourselves can preoccupy us. It is important for you to clarify via technology the intent and purpose of the communication sent. This is true for both voice and written communication.

- the meaning perspective of communication between and among virtual team members reflects an interaction between feelings, thoughts and behaviours. Virtual team members report that they are often ambivalent about expressing themselves accurately. This is especially true when cultural and language sensitivities are active in a team. The result is that you may find yourself speaking obscurely about ideas and even less clearly about your feelings. In some cultures team members may have been conditioned to speak indirectly on many topics or not to express their feelings.

■ engagement versus freedom: some virtual team members will be more self-directed whilst others will require direction and structure. Working virtually means a change in routine and the need for instant access to be redefined. You have the choice of the level of engagement you have with others as well as the way you organise your time and work on a virtual team. As a manager you may need to provide a more structured set of work requirements for those people requiring direction whilst leaving self-directed members to get on with the work.

Productive virtual teams have an agreed set of mega-communication protocols where they give each other and the leader permission to do a 'perspective check' when they feel they are becoming disconnected from the content of the work. These may include: regular briefings supported by highly structured meeting agendas; capacity and workload agreements; priority setting and time management; delegation and responsibility charting; 'stealth' sessions; and, meeting and agenda management.

Virtual teams often report that their meetings (via video-conferences, telephone, social media or other technologies) are the most difficult part of the experience. The issue for discussion may not be the major concern of the team, as people rarely initiate conversations focused on the matters of greatest concern. Everyone 'travels incognito' to varying degrees. Virtual team working can provide the opportunity for team members to hide behind issues or difficulties and avoid dealing with their concerns about a task or obligation. The result may be solutions to minor problems while the more difficult issues and concerns are not addressed. How often have you been in a team meeting where seemingly petty issues are discussed ad infinitum, and a major concern only mentioned at the last minute or even after the meeting? As a manager and leader of virtual teams you should expect team members to support a 'perspective check' in order to provide an opportunity to address concerns simmering just below the surface.

In chapter 3, we noted the importance of communicating a shared vision and goals, giving the team direction and purpose within the larger organisation. It is important for you as a manager to state simply and 'communicate' a shared vision and goals for the mandate of the virtual team. Productive virtual teams can then re-define their purpose

Figure 6 Keys to managing virtual team meetings

1. Do the detailed work via email before the meeting

2. Focus, focus, focus – keep the agenda short and specific

3. Include relationship building activities at the beginning and the end of the meeting

4. Ensure everyone participates and that all opinions are voiced

5. Include a time for difficult topics – make it possible to 'say the unsayable'

6. Have ground rules for dealing with unhelpful language and behaviours

7. Commit to openness

8. Take time to check understanding on all decisions, however minor

9. Respect the time zones of members and their sense of time – always be punctual, on time

10. If people don't look forward to the meeting, you're doing it wrong!

Adapted from D Clutterbuck, 2004

and goals within the limits of the strategic goals of the business. The term 'communicate' is stressed as it is more than just developing a vision and a set of goals. It reflects the normal behaviours expected, and a specific, clearly defined set of outcomes that are meaningful to virtual team members, and help define the level of commitment and energy required to be productive.

Trust: the dynamics of working with others unseen over periods of time, the tendency of technology to de-personalise relationships and the requirements of many adults to support their work relationships with some degree of emotional connection, place the role of trust at the centre of virtual team working. In the life of any team, disagreements, misunderstandings and mistakes will occur. And there may be an element of suspicion by managers that virtual and home-based working equate to slacking or abuse of agreements. So, trust plays an important role in virtual teams where ambiguity is high.

"Lack of trust can undermine every other precaution taken to ensure successful virtual work arrangements"

W Cascio, 2001

In order to build the requisite level of trust when working as a member of a virtual team, it is essential to foster working relationships that are characterised by a culturally appropriate level of openness and willingness to share, and learn how to address the emotional needs, with flexibility in approach to solutions and outcomes. In general, virtual teams operate with few rules, norms or precedents for how to work effectively as a unit. Fostering a willingness to share information across cultural and technological boundaries, addressing disagreements and problems immediately they occur, and supporting a level of communication with respect and understanding, enable you to push beyond the inevitable conflicts that emerge in any situation where people must work together.

It is crucial to remember that people do not automatically work well together as a group or team despite a common culture or work setting. In particular, the use of technology creates unique challenges for the work of virtual teams. It may, necessarily, de-personalise conflict resolution and problem-solving, since when disagreements surface the use of the written medium coupled with time delays between communications, de-personalise the situation. This suggests that a sufficient level of trust and openness, together with the safety of distance and time, can be a benefit to working on relationship issues. Collaboration flourishes in a climate of trust.

A critical way for you to develop trust is to involve virtual team members in defining the vision, reviewing the strategy and planning deliverables, even on teams with short delivery schedules. This is especially important when team members do not have the opportunity to meet in person.

Take the following example: a global technology consulting company with a strong, tightly-knit family based culture, deployed a virtual team of volunteer technical and marketing members to deliver a one-off integrated client solution in the record time of three weeks. The members with the necessary expertise were located in Europe and the United States and had not worked together before. The leader of the team was based in California. Throughout the three week deployment, the team interacted daily via videoconference. When the project commenced the team leader decided that, due to the tight delivery schedule, he would define the tasks, establish work schedules and milestones for each phase of the delivery, and sought minimal feedback from team members. Videoconference meeting times were scheduled for 09.00 California time with no consideration of time zone difference. During the three weeks, the full team was never present for video conferences, technical problems diminished voice and picture quality, other work continued during the videoconferences, deadlines were missed by the US-based members, and conflicts over meeting times (due to time zone differences) were not addressed. The project was delivered on time by the European team but did not meet full customer specifications.

When the work of the virtual team is only performance-based rather than relationship-based, building trust is difficult. Trust takes time to develop in any team setting. Taking the time up front to engage the team in the work of the deliverables will save time later.

Relationship building: selection of employees for virtual teams often lacks any structure, but it does require thoughtful consideration. Productive virtual team members usually have a good understanding of how the organisation works, know the key stakeholder relationships essential for getting the work done, have the ability to assess what is needed to make things happen, and are flexible and adaptable. The critical ingredient here is the ability to establish and maintain relationships or networking.

To this end we have identified a set of relationship building competencies and requirements that individuals need to perform effectively as a virtual team. These include:
- problem-solving and decision-making
- interpersonal and diversity/cultural awareness
- enthusiasm and commitment for working on a virtual team
- time and support of management to contribute
- a high degree of self-direction and motivation
- an ability and desire to use technology as a source for working.

Since virtual teams tend to operate in an environment where few rules and precedents may be available, leveraging relationships is often key for getting the work done. Insufficient knowledge of the experience and skills of other team members will prevent you from tapping into your virtual colleagues' knowledge base.

For example, an international software development organisation, with multiple virtual product development and project support teams, began to miss critical development deadlines with key customers. The teams, together with management, discovered that team members were not really fully aware of the competencies and experience of their colleagues, and therefore did not consult with them. They preferred to work on the development locally, citing that they did not want to bother colleagues the other side of the world. These roadblocks to the various team members' mutual sense of community and trust were addressed through online meetings and sharing individual biographies. These quickly helped them get back on schedule.

The difficulty with sustaining relationships when working in virtual teams lies in a basic human need to have time and contact to build trust and comfort with others. The most significant barrier to success is the lack of face-to-face contact, particularly in the early stages. The level of commitment is directly related to the level of contact. Audio- and video-conferencing help in sustaining the basic relationship development, but do not replace the need for occasional face-to-face contact. This may be the major drawback to the use of virtual teams where intensive work among the team members is required.

The importance of the emotional dimension of relationship building, mentioned earlier, is probably the most difficult for you and your organisation to assess. In the emotional realm of human interactions, the notion of logic, rational thinking and common sense take on a subtler, less concrete nature. As a manager and leader of a virtual team you are encouraged to develop your 'third ear' to understand the undercurrents that may be influencing the work. Learning to listen to internal discourse, or self-talk, is the most effective way to listen with the 'third ear'.

You are sitting in a virtual team review session via *Webex* with team colleagues. During the meeting you notice by the voice and choice of language that a colleague on your team sounds tense and appears to be frustrated and impatient. You ask this colleague if there is anything they require or if any issues remain to be addressed. She declines to add any more detail to the discussion. You might overlook this situation as an event of insignificance. Indeed, if it is noted at all, you may dismiss such an event as a result of cultural or personality issues. The reaction of the colleague can be reviewed from a number of different perspectives. In this example, the critical factor for the virtual team leader and members to develop a 'third ear', is to attend to the observation and take what are deemed appropriate steps to manage the colleague.

Whilst no clear-cut best practice is available to assist in relationship building for virtual teams, various actions by the manager and virtual team members can be beneficial (see Figure 7).

Figure 7 Relationship building strategies

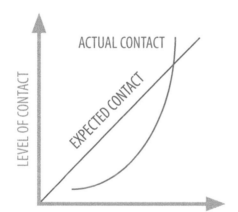

- support sharing of problems and conflicts related to work
- establish formal communication controls
- encourage off-line communication
- reward successes/examine failures as a team
- agree dependencies
- clarify expectations, time/location/frequency of meetings
- agree autonomy
- define standards of team quality, performance and feedback
- assess technologies
- agree project management tools
- agree evaluation criteria
- schedule face-to-face meetings at regular intervals

Whatever the type of virtual team, we suggest the key behaviour drivers for success are:

- speaking openly and clearly
- knowing each other's strengths and weaknesses and how each other thinks
- valuing difference
- sharing knowledge and expertise
- trusting each other's ability and goodwill
- generating enthusiasm for the challenge and from interacting with each other – the 'fizz and the buzz'.

How do we implement relationships?

At the inception of virtual teams, you are encouraged to agree protocols for the following:

- to provide face-time and frequency of face-to-face meetings
- to maintain motivation and commitment and engagement
- to respect different time zones
- to encourage relationship building
- to manage conflict, problem solving and decision making.

QUESTIONS FOR YOU TO CONSIDER

1. How do you create and 'communicate' a shared vision and common direction for virtual teams?

2. Is management able to clearly articulate the expectations and accountabilities of team members in team performance?

3. How do you develop trust with staff working in virtual teams?

4. What tools are at your disposal to support comfort, relationship building and trust on your virtual team?

THE WIS STORY – PART FOUR

Face-time was key in the early stages of the project. After the initial face-to-face meeting with team members and key stakeholders, the team and their manager got together in one location every few weeks, in addition to having their weekly videoconference meetings as a group and regular email contact. The team manager also regularly contacted each team member individually to continue to build up their relationship and ensure each person could express any individual issues or concerns they might have that they felt they could not express in front of the other members of the team.

Developing trust with and within the team was paramount to keeping the KSI project moving forward. Team members were encouraged to be open and respectful in their communications, to share information, and to be flexible in understanding others from different cultural backgrounds. This created a positive and cooperative mood amongst team members. They learned to be clear in both written and verbal communication using simple unambiguous language, to appreciate the nuances of body language and tone of voice, and to check that colleagues, particularly those whose mother tongue was not English, understood their messages. When inevitably disagreements occurred they were shared by the team, to come up with mutually acceptable solutions.

case study the WIS story

chapter 6

technology

> *"Sometimes the best use of technology isn't to enhance a product or make it easier to stay in touch with customers, but simply to make it easier to stay in touch with other people on your own staff."*

John Case & Karen Carney, 1996 (Open-Book)

D ue to the variety of locations of your virtual team members, communication technology must be evaluated honestly for its suitability as a communication tool. Virtual team members need to clarify and critically evaluate the accessibility, viability and credibility of communication alternatives.

The choice of communication tools establishes the foundations for virtual team success. Whilst some variations do exist, most people find the most effective technologies to be social media, email and telephone and to a lesser extent the more sophisticated technologies, such as videoconferencing. Most virtual team members like to use two or more technologies. However, real-time communication technologies are not essential to team success.

"The rise of the internet, the creation of a global fibre-optic network, and the rapid development of long distance communication technologies has made it very easy for people all over the world to work together. It has created a global platform that has allowed more people to plug and play, collaborate and compete, share knowledge and share work, than anything we have ever seen in the history of the world."

Thomas Friedman, 2005 (journalist and author)

Imagine yourself managing a virtual team in the early 1980s. What technologies would have been available to you then? Fax certainly, and maybe telex. Mobile telephony was in its infancy, and email just a dream. The landline telephone was the most prevalent technology available and used, although it was not widely available in some geographical locations. And a lot of time and resources were spent by managers travelling to many places around the world to meet their team members, to discuss project progress and to resolve issues. A colleague recalls a project team leader based in the UK undergoing a day trip to India to meet the local virtual team members to resolve a strategic issue critical to the success of a project!

Today, technology is the key that drives virtual team working, particularly as it is available 24/7 via the web. You can use a variety of technology tools, depending on availability. In general, the main technology tools currently used are:

- smart phones
- email
- instant messaging
- VoIP eg *Skype, Webex*
- fax
- video conferencing: a powerful tool as few of the facial cues, body language indications or voice intonations and modulations from normal face-to-face communication are lost. However, there is a lack

of eye contact as individuals look at the camera. And some people can be quite self conscious before a camera

- collaborative software: dedicated information and file sharing systems
- online discussion forums/'war rooms': virtual spaces where team members collaborate to discuss, coordinate and accomplish their activities. They facilitate document sharing, exchanges of information real-time, online discussions, sharing work plans, and monitoring the progress of the team's activities
- shared virtual work spaces: posting work in progress electronically for all team members to view before, for instance, a teleconference, drop box or virtual office software
- communities of practice
- intranet and extranet
- social networking, blogging, wikis and specific online chat rooms. Such tools are increasingly used for getting to know colleagues and relationship building. Social networking sites pose a challenge to organisations. Confidentiality, security, legal and ethical requirements influence the viability and relevance as a tool for working remotely. A policy on use and access is necessary if social media is to be a component of working virtually.

This is not an exhaustive list, of course, and technological developments will inevitably supplement and even supplant existing tools. There is currently a significant trend towards 'cloud-computing' and 'desktop virtualisation', where everything is hosted by a third party and accessed over the internet. Another trend is towards 'unified communications' (UC). UC integrates services that provide both real-time communication (eg telephone, instant messaging, videoconferencing) and non-real-time communication (eg email, fax, voicemail) into one user interface. Any technology that helps virtual teams work more effectively and efficiently should be considered. In 2010 Cisco carried out a study of employees working from home part of the week and using the company's 'virtual office' equipment. Findings showed that they were some 50% more productive than when working in the office.

However, the choice of technology needs to be consistent with the ability of your organisation to support and sustain the delivery. Choice is also influenced by legal and administrative concerns for privacy, storage of data, security and organisation firewall requirements. We advise all virtual teams to identify a technology 'advocate', who is your direct source of support and advice on technology issues. Virtual teams are vulnerable to the problems associated with managing technology issues in organisations. In South Korea, an initiative is under way to create 'smart work' centres with laptops and mobile internet devices, to enable 30% of employees to work nearer home *(Korea Times, 2010)*. And in Europe and the USA there are already networks of smart work centres, particularly in the Netherlands, with the purpose of reducing environmental pollution through reduced travel. *(Maitland and Thomson, 2011)*.

In the 1990s, the joint military services in the US started redesigning health care delivery up to 2020, and it was imperative that the project included a wide range of individuals located across the United States. They also recognised that this virtual project team would require access to resources from research bodies, to the latest from telemedicine and to new approaches to nursing education.

Reassigning more than 200 people to Washington, DC, for a one-year project was not going to be feasible. It soon became apparent that the only way to successfully implement this project was via an intranet.

A face-to-face kick-off meeting was held over three days, which included the project team of more than 200 people representing the three services, the Veterans Administration and experts from academia and the private sector. At the end of the meeting, each member of the project team returned home and participated in this project via a private workspace accessible via the internet.

Participants in the project were assigned to teams focused on different issues. In turn, each team had access to a private web-based conference where specifics around their issue were discussed. In order to provide a way for the individual teams to share ideas about cross-cutting themes, web-based conferences were also established. All members of the project team had access to the on-line resources of research bodies and to news and information online from various services.

The virtual project team worked together via the internet for nine months. The result was a success and the internet-based project team of more than 200 individuals completed a set of scenarios on health care delivery systems for the 21st century for top management review. *(L Kimball, Group Jazz)*.

From our experience of virtual team working, it appears that written communication, including texting, tweeting and social media, is preferred for most of the work of virtual teams. It can de-personalise communication, which is particularly useful when disagreements and the demands of the task create conflict amongst team members. It also offers a breathing space to reflect and examine the content of a communication. Such reflection time is often missing from the intensity of face-to-face or telephone communication. Written communication can provide the foundation for team members to focus better on the tasks of their team's work, especially when a team is spread out over several geographical regions.

Technology can make or break the success of a virtual team. You and your virtual team must assess the available technology and its ability to provide the level and scope of communication required to deliver the performance. In some locations internet access may be poor, intermittent or restricted; mobile telephone signals may also be difficult in some regions, and landlines non-existent. Choosing the right technologies and the technology strategy need to be based on rigorously assessing not only operational needs but also individual and virtual team potential to use the tools for flexible working. All virtual teams need an agreed technology plan for the type and scope of communication technology they will use.

You and your organisation should also build contingency plans for communication and the deployment of expertise required for all virtual teams. If you do not, this is what can happen. In the midst of a short-term, business critical project for a global telephony company, a series of typhoons battered the regions of the Pacific Rim, ranging from Hong Kong to Tokyo. The storms eliminated basic electrical and telephone services for several weeks in many areas. Team members in these regions were isolated from their colleagues in the rest of Asia and Europe, depriving them of critical data essential to the delivery of the project. With no back-up plan, the team missed the deadline resulting in the loss of a market leadership position.

How do we implement technology?

At the inception of virtual teams, you are encouraged to agree protocols for the following:

- key tools for communication including a common set of agreed technologies and forms of communication
- gaps in use and coverage of tools and available remedies
- investment requirements
- back-up systems
- assumptions and expectations for the level and scope of use
- technology stakeholders and their abilities to assist in everyday and crisis situations.

 QUESTIONS FOR YOU TO CONSIDER

1. What are the technological limitations and opportunities influencing standard work practice in your organisation?

2. How will these limitations and opportunities impact the ability of your virtual teams to sustain and deliver results?

3. What are the preferred communication links between virtual team members?

THE WIS STORY – PART FIVE

At the outset of the KSI project, the team manager was able to bring in an expert from the IT department, to advise on technology issues and support the technology plan. A survey was carried out throughout the organisation worldwide to confirm the technologies being used regionally, and to ascertain any problems in connectivity, local contingency plans, and any needs for investment to update technological requirements.

The team members also exchanged ideas on their preferred uses of technology. The vast majority voted for email as the basic communications tool, and a dedicated intranet site to share and coordinate their work to enable them to collaborate effectively. Videoconferencing facilities were considered essential for weekly team meetings, between their face-to-face monthly meetings. Team members were also given the go-ahead to use social media to get to know their team colleagues better and help build their relationships.

Of course, at the same time the opportunity was taken to carry out an audit of the various software being used in the organisation across the world, to make sure that the knowledge management database under development could be accessed easily, and if not, appropriate technical solutions put in place.

Following the IT expert's report, additional investment was obtained from the Finance Director, so that the technology plan could be implemented fully to provide really effective support for the project.

case study   the WIS story

chapter 7

understanding

"All people are the same. It's only their habits that are so different."

Confucius

nderstanding means being able to figure out simple ways to communicate about something in language that makes sense and is meaningful to others. In the introduction we noted that virtual teams are unique and require managers and team members to be aware of and communicate this uniqueness to others. This is especially evident when we look at the role that culture, from team to national culture, plays in the work of virtual teams. The work requires members to be aware of the visible and invisible expressions of culture in the life of the team. In this chapter we focus on the challenges in understanding cross-cultural awareness in virtual teams within and outside the organisation.

To 'understand' the various dimensions is like peeling an onion – when you peel away the outer layers you reveal the inner depths, reaching the centre that represents the core values of a culture. Aspects of culture that significantly impact cross-cultural communication include, amongst others, ideology, socialisation, language, body language, use of space, concept of time, social organisation. Learned behaviours, automatic responses and psychological predispositions will necessarily influence our style of communication, what we communicate and how we react to communication, especially when technology is involved.

A general overview of the interplay between culture and communication is presented in Figure 8 (opposite). Note that the term 'context culture' is the basic element influencing the communication requirements of virtual team members. In this environment, we define context culture as the expression of behavioural, psychological and cognitive dimensions informing cultural preferences.

People from high context cultures tend to be indirect and formal in their communication style, combining verbal and nonverbal messages to convey the meaning. Their cultures are more group-focused than individual-focused, and therefore they live within societal norms that are less focused on individual needs. An important aim of their communication style is to maintain harmony, so not everything is said, but rather much can be implied. People who prefer an indirect communication style will avoid dealing directly with conflict, but rather handle issues privately, through a third party or through passive resistance. Any disagreement will be handled in a manner that causes the least amount of open dissension. This style is concerned about 'saving face', dealing with an issue in a way that does not embarrass anyone in public or cause them to lose respect, with blame not being apportioned directly but rather alluded to. Consequently, it is important for you to have excellent listening and observation skills when interacting with such people. Examples of high context, group-focused cultures are most countries in Asia, the Middle East, Africa, South America.

Some years ago, three internationally renowned companies from Germany, Japan and the USA decided to form a joint venture. During the negotiations, the German team were surprised to find Japanese managers closing their eyes and seeming to sleep during meetings (a common practice with Japanese managers when talk does not concern them). The Japanese, who normally work in big groups, found

Figure 8 Cultural and virtual team communication

high context cultures	low context cultures
COMMUNICATION	
polite	open
respectful	true
integration by similarities/harmony	integration by authenticity
indirect and implicit messages	direct, simple, clear messages
high use of non-verbal communication	low use of non-verbal communication
low reliance on written communication	high reliance on written communication
DISADVANTAGES	
May be viewed by low context cultures as:	May be viewed by high context cultures as:
hiding information	impolite
insensitive to nuances of language	diminishing social/cultural feel of team
too formal	giving confusing messages
arrogant	naive
using time inefficiently	impersonal and directive
focusing on situation versus outcome	lacking self-discipline
considering process over content	too fast
too slow	
PREFERRED CHANNELS OF COMMUNICATION	
non-virtual meetings · net meetings · video conferences · audio conferences · fax · email	
high context cultures	low context cultures

Source: adapted from Hofstede, 1991

it uncomfortable to sit in small, individual offices and speak English. The Americans complained that the Germans planned too much and that the Japanese, who like to review ideas constantly, would not make clear decisions. This is a good example of lack of cultural awareness by the three organisations involved.

The communication style of people from low context cultures tends to be direct and informal. They rely on the precise meaning of the words they use and prefer explicit communication where words convey most of the message. They prefer written communication as they do not feel the need to include the subtleness of nonverbal communication. Conflict is dealt with head-on and using statements such as "Let's get everything out into the open". They believe that if you discuss everything you can resolve the conflict, and that it is better to say what needs to be said. Examples of low context, individual-focused cultures are the USA, Germany, Switzerland and the Scandinavian countries.

At an international management conference in Europe, the American organisers amused and annoyed the European audience by going over the conference sessions in detail, spelling out what was clearly already outlined in the conference programme. They also went as far as to put in writing how the American participants were supposed to behave with an international audience.

So what do direct and indirect communicators think of each other? Direct communicators tend to consider indirect communicators to be evasive, dishonest, unable to take a stand, having no opinion, and increasing tension by not dealing with issues directly. Indirect communicators are inclined to think direct communicators are insensitive, have no tact and are boorish, insulting, harsh, and increase tension by dealing with issues in a direct manner. For instance, in communications between American and French people, Americans, with their direct approach, generally start from the assumption that the listener knows nothing. The French, on the other hand, with their indirect approach, start from the assumption that the listener knows everything. What tends to happen is that the French will perceive that the Americans think they are stupid because they start explaining everything, and vice versa.

A major challenge for you with virtual teams composed of speakers of different languages is that the building of trust and relationships is largely language dependent. Language diversity has a significant impact on socialisation processes and team building, influencing both communication and mutual perceptions. Even English native speakers from different countries can encounter obstacles. It is essential for you to develop an appreciation of the effort required from all virtual team members who do not speak the language of choice of your organisation. For those members who do not speak more than one language, the demands of working as a virtual team can be daunting.

With communication styles differing widely among various cultures, it is easy to be led into misrepresenting what is being communicated. Even if someone from another country speaks English, it is not going to be the same English that is spoken elsewhere. This makes non-verbal communication, such as pauses, silence, body language and expressions which differ between cultures, more important in virtual teams, and should be known and understood by other team members. Remember that silence may not reflect a lack of interest but may simply represent time needed to think or just waiting for a formal invitation to speak. And differences in body language observed during videoconferencing can be misinterpreted.

Two main cultural issues that surface in virtual teams are a false perception of similarity and differing perceptions of work and team work. The perceived familiarity and similarity across English-speaking countries can lead you into a false sense of confidence and into failing to perceive that you may not be culturally similar. This can have a negative impact on business communication processes and personal relationships. The value of work and team work may also differ greatly between countries.

If you were born and brought up in the UK and the USA you will tend to be more individualistic. If you were born and brought up in China and India, however, you are more focused on collective efforts. When communicating electronically, people from low context/individualistic cultures tend to be more ready to trust other individuals than people from high context/collectivist cultures. Such differences can make it difficult for you to determine the cause of a problem between virtual team members, since it is not easy to distinguish between cultural and personal factors. Cultural difference and personality difference are closely linked. As long as you recognise individual variation in personality traits, you can appreciate the national core values within a culture.

When it comes to making decisions, people from different cultures may take different views on what constitutes a decision. For example, an American may emerge from a discussion understanding that everyone has now agreed to a firm set of actions and responsibilities. However, a French person may believe that the broad principles have been set out but they are free to interpret these in their own way. And a Japanese person may feel that the process of decision making has only just started!

"There are companies (and even regions) that revel in top- down decision handouts, while others believe in a bottom-up approach; teamwork is emphasised at places, while individualised decision-making is the norm elsewhere. This has a profound influence on distributed teams, since different parts of the team adopt the culture that is physically closest to them. If parts of a team employ different ways of decision-making, it can be very disruptive to team-functioning."

R Dileepan, Mastek

Working across time zones and with countries with different working practices may also create challenges for you. Setting up meetings and video conferences with virtual team members situated in differing time zones can cause difficulties in getting everyone together at the same time. In addition energy levels will be different amongst team members, as for some it will be morning while for others it will be the end of the day. And not all cultures work on a Monday to Friday schedule, but rather Saturday to Wednesday, or Sunday to Thursday. So, by respecting time zones and varying the days and times of meetings, so that it is not always early morning or late evening for the same team members, you will have more effective interactions.

For example, a small, provincial-based virtual team dedicated to dealing with client emergencies on a continuous basis in a global professional services company, reported diminished coverage on

Thursdays and Fridays in parts of the Middle East. Team members were not available at short notice when required. Due to cultural practices, Thursdays and Fridays were set aside as days for religious retreat.

Indeed, cultural differences are not just a matter of demographics. In practice cultural values can vary significantly among team members within the same country, for example in the USA, a country populated to a large extent by people whose ancestral culture developed elsewhere. This impacts the communication, relationship building, and our notion of the nature and role of leadership. When we ask members of virtual teams to identify and describe the top three characteristics of successful virtual team leaders, divergence across cultures is common, reflecting the values of the culture brought to the team.

It is important for you to discuss the potential impact of cultural and diversity influences on the work of your virtual teams. The work of David Rees around cultural fluency (see Figure 9 below) captures the value of having these discussions. Whilst this may be difficult for some individuals, the ability to highlight potential areas of conflict is essential to the work of the team. So, when you, as a manager of a virtual team, face situations of diversity and cultural difference you need to become

Figure 9 **The culturally fluent manager**

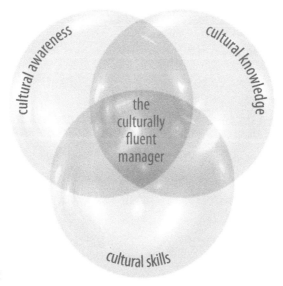

Source: Rees, 2002

aware of and understand shared sets of values, attitudes and behaviours – to become culturally fluent.

People vary in how they deal with other cultures. Individuals with high cultural intelligence look for clues to identify shared understanding in people from the same cultural background, learn the customs and gestures of those from other cultures and therefore act more like them, thus increasing understanding, trust, openness and communication between cultures.

Try out the assessment at the end of this chapter to find out your level of cultural fluency.

How do we implement understanding?

At the inception of virtual teams, you are encouraged to agree protocols for the following:

- the language to be used for communication across the team and that enhances understanding
- learning about culturally specific behaviours
- exploring ways of developing 'culturally fluent' habits
- managing cultural and diversity issues.

QUESTIONS FOR YOU TO CONSIDER

1. Does your management identify and support local cultural and diversity values and norms as a condition for performance?

2. What are the organisational, regional or national cultural issues your team may face in achieving its deliverable?

3. What cultural barriers may emerge as a result of the virtual team working together?

4. What tools do you have at your disposal to manage the cultural issues?

5. Are virtual teams encouraged to coordinate activities around cultural and diversity requirements?

6. What technical tools are available to overcome language barriers and does management support contributions from members where the language of business may not be their native tongue?

THE WIS STORY – PART SIX

The KSI project team was multi-cultural in nature, with members located in Africa, Asia, the Middle East, Europe and North and South America. To help team members understand each other better, cross-cultural communication training sessions were organised. These took place at the monthly face-to-face meetings, thus providing individuals with a practical setting in which to use their newly acquired skills, and resolve any misunderstandings face-to-face. Such training proved invaluable to the team, so much so that the project team had it rolled out to the KSI stakeholders also. Since the company's global language of communication was international English, opportunities were also provided for individuals to improve their written and spoken English.

It was decided that the project would be coordinated out of the UK, since time-wise (GMT) it was well located between Singapore and the west coast of the USA. The team manager scheduled the days and times of meetings and videoconference calls with input from team members, to ensure varied timings to suit different regions and national and religious holidays. This meant a huge planning effort, but was appreciated by team members and contributed to a real sense of team cohesion and collaboration.

case study the WIS story

EXERCISE	ASSESSING YOUR PERSONAL LEVEL OF CULTURAL FLUENCY							
	Total non-cultural fluency	Some awareness	Active awareness	Some understanding	Active understanding	Some skills	Culturally skilled	Culturally fluent
Understanding how, when and where to apply the awareness, knowledge and skills I have								GLOBAL ROAMER
I love travelling, got lots of experience, and like to communicate in the way they do							SEASONED TRANS-NATIONALIST	
I enjoy multicultural experiences and try to 'act local'						RAPPORT BUILDER		
The reasons for cultural differences are understood					LEARNED TRAVELLER			
I can clearly see cultural differences, I know some of the reasons for this				WILLING LEARNER				
Cultures are different, I don't understand why but I'm interested			INQUISITIVE TOURIST					
I know people are different but I don't see the need to change my behaviour		DAY TRIPPER						
No knowledge, awareness or skills for dealing with other cultures	STAY AT HOME							

Adapted from *Cross-Cultural Team Building* (Berger, 1996)

EXERCISE — MEASURING YOUR CULTURAL INTELLIGENCE

Rate the extent to which you agree with each statement, using the following scale:

1 strongly disagree   **2** disagree   **3** neutral   **4** agree   **5** strongly agree

[ ] Before I interact with people from a new culture I ask myself what I hope to achieve

[ ] If I encounter something unexpected while working in a new culture I use this experience to work out new ways to approach other cultures in the future

[ ] I plan how I'm going to relate to people from a different culture before I meet them

[ ] When I come into a new cultural situation, I can immediately sense whether something is going well or something is wrong

[ ] Total ÷ 4 = [ ] cognitive cultural intelligence

[ ] It's easy for me to change my body language to suit people from a different culture

[ ] I can alter my expression when a cultural encounter requires it

[ ] I modify my speech style to suit people from a different culture

[ ] I easily change the way I act when a cross-cultural encounter seems to require it

[ ] Total ÷ 4 = [ ] physical cultural intelligence

[ ] I have confidence that I can deal well with people from a different culture

[ ] I am certain that I can befriend people whose cultural backgrounds are different from mine

[ ] I can adapt to the lifestyle of a different culture with relative ease

[ ] I am confident that I can deal with a cultural situation that is unfamiliar

[ ] Total ÷ 4 = [ ] emotional/motivational cultural intelligence

Generally, an average of less than 3 indicates an area for improvement, while an average of 4.5 or more reflects a true Cultural Intelligence strength

Based on *Cultural Intelligence, HBR* (October 2004) Earley & Mosakowski

chapter 8

alignment

"Willingness to change is a strength, even if it means plunging part of the company into total confusion for a while."

Jack Welch

lignment means providing a relatively straightforward path to goals and taking decisions that provide virtual teams with some level of structure and support. A participant in a recent virtual team's workshop made an amusing, yet salient, point when she commented, *"Leading a virtual team is like herding cats... chaos in all directions!"* You may dismiss as impracticable the idea of 'herding cats', yet can it be accomplished? To do so requires you to re-think the way you understand how these creatures operate and interact with their environment, and the actions you need to take to manage the chaos. Herding cats is possible according to a veterinary friend!

Are you actually able to manage effectively in a virtual environment? Is it possible to achieve a level of alignment among members when the environment may not be conducive to working in a virtual manner? Like 'herding cats', to lead virtual teams successfully requires you to re-think the way you understand traditional ways that a collection of individuals functions to achieve results – how teams operate and individuals interact within a team in a virtual environment.

For example, do the assumptions you use to define effective team work hold true in virtual teams? Does the way you think about an intact or co-located team hold true for virtual teams? Are the assumptions you hold about the amount of information the team requires to be successful the same for a virtual team? What do you, as a team member and manager, actually need to know about other members to be successful as a virtual team? Is the frequency and style of communication the same for virtual teams as for intact teams? Do the same tools used to manage conflicts, take decisions and deliver information to key stakeholders, work with virtual teams? What assumptions are informing your view of how to work as a member or leader of a virtual team?

A compass is oriented to magnetic north and provides a general orientation for action. If a team understands its magnetic north, alignment and coordination for action may be easier to manage. A variety of information drives alignment. And in virtual teams, thinking differently about how teams operate and individuals interact within a team in a virtual environment is necessary.

Alignment requires a clear, easily understood and communicated vision / magnetic north for a virtual team. This provides direction and allows you to choose a diverse range of tools to evaluate information and your own thoughts in a disciplined way. A team may spend a great deal of time struggling with an issue, decision or a particular question using established organisational systems and tools, when in fact reformulating or redesigning these is required before progress can occur. Failing to consider the limitations and opportunities in current systems, structures, processes and relationships hinders alignment. When developed by a team, the most viable and reliable systems, structures, processes and relationships can be agreed in order to sustain alignment. For instance, due to divergent business goals across a multi-functional team, members may feel compromised or torn between local business unit concerns and the larger strategic requirements of the virtual team. Alignment provides options and choices for managing the tensions generated by divergent business goals.

In most cases your systems, structures, processes and relationships will need to be tweaked, re-aligned and adapted to remove potential blockages to alignment on virtual teams. Sharing information, knowledge and wisdom via online communities of practice, for instance, is important to virtual team members to keep them up-to-date on what is happening in other parts of the organisation. Or maybe you will find that the use of social media is helpful. This may require a 'culture shift' in your organisation from a 'command and control' type of culture to a culture of trust. Such a transition in organisation culture takes time and requires the active commitment of senior leaders, managers and virtual team members. Whatever you do, you need to 'walk the talk'!

As a manager and virtual team member, you require senior management to confront the paradox of ambiguity and lack of control in a business climate. This means recognising and accepting the complexity of the environment in which virtual teams operate, understanding how the organisation gets things done, who the key stakeholders are and where power rests - who make things happen. Within this environment, it is essential for you to work with key stakeholders to influence when required and to ensure that virtual team members are supported when dual commitments and divided loyalties emerge.

Achieving the appropriate alignment requires effort that will sustain itself over time through management actions and significant cultural changes. Many team members can feel quite vulnerable, and anxious about losing their sources of power, information, comfort, resource and status. They may therefore demonstrate a tendency to resist any change or not support the effort. To proceed as smoothly as possible through the alignment process it will help you to have a map to predict the path. Moving along the path may take from a few hours to several weeks, or even months in some cases. We use the Transition Curve (see Figure 10 overleaf). It provides such a path and has four major phases: step 1: assumptions checking; step 2: resisting; step 3: challenging; step 4: thriving.

Step 1: assumptions checking: defining assumptions about the nature and role of alignment is a three step process for teams:

- as a virtual team, what assumptions do you bring to the table to define success and failure as a team? Be specific, focused and intentional in debating this question.

Figure 10 **Transition curve**

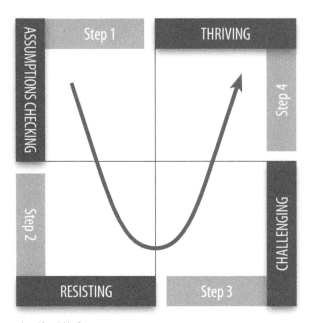

adapted from Kubler-Ross

- reconsider the assumptions by considering the opposite assumption. For instance, if your team identifies the following assumption: *"we will only get marginal or nominal support for our work by management"* the opposite assumption is *"we will get the full support of management for this project."*
- follow up with this question: What evidence or data do you have to support the opposite assumption? This is a compelling question for it asks the team to consider information outside the comfort zone of the team.

Without exception, this discussion generates discomfort or bias towards a point of view or perspective. In our work, we often see resistance to this type of discussion as it challenges uncritically assimilated bias and inferences. This enables you to protect yourself from being overwhelmed. By examining your assumptions about the alignment process, sooner or later the impact and reality will catch up with you and you move to Step 2.

Step 2: resisting: here things seem to get worse. You may spend time looking for someone or something to challenge the assumptions, often expressing a complaint about the process, assumptions, or the work relationship. You may feel all sorts of physical, emotional and mental symptoms, and even discuss your challenge with the team.

Here is the critical action required of you as a team leader - consistently and firmly support debating and conversing about the assumptions informing the views of team members. If supported, this discussion allows individuals and organisations to emerge, breathe a sigh of relief and move into a more positive, hopeful, future-focused phase. A noticeable shift occurs that lets you know you are going to make it through. It can be as subtle as just feeling better or more obvious like sleeping through the night for the first time since the alignment process started.

The sense of 'shifting' differs for each person, but you will know when it happens. The shift results in allowing you to begin thinking about the future and accepting the transition.

Step 3: challenging: what emerges first is the energy to explore and discover new ways. You will start clarifying goals, assessing resources, exploring alternatives, and experimenting with new possibilities. You will feel motivated to swing into action without trying too quickly to find 'the right way'. You should resist stopping too soon by accepting something less than you are capable of. This is a period of high energy. Your creativity will be at its peak. It is also a time of wild shifts and unfocused intensity.

Curiosity is essential in this step. Engaging in inquisitive thinking, such as exploration, investigation and learning, asking questions and considering new possibilities, reflect curiosity. It is at the core of reconsidering those systems, structures, processes and relationships that allow virtual teams to thrive.

Step 4: thriving: at the core of a high performing virtual team is a sense of discovery, confidence to explore new ways of doing things and adapting to new situations. The team has the experience of making steady progress towards its mission and goals, recognising that set-backs and conflicts are inevitable, and that maintaining a sense of proportion and balance are the hallmarks of thriving.

A key to thriving is the virtual team's performance measures. We often find that virtual team work is expected and promoted, yet no recognition or reward for virtual team working is embedded in the performance management system of an organisation. The result is team members feel their efforts have gone unnoticed and consequently their levels of commitment may decrease. Successful virtual teams are supported by a performance management system that is focused on outcomes, and places a level of value on both individual and team performance. Within this context, the virtual team is different from the sum of its parts, yet it is intimately linked to individual performance.

The Transition Curve never ends. You keep moving in a rhythm of change as long as you live, facing new challenges and crises. It is common to have several transition rhythms going at the same time. It is important to know how many personal and organisational transitions you are going through at any one time, so that you can be careful not to overwhelm yourself.

It is helpful to increase transition awareness amongst employees and managers at all levels. This will enable individual virtual team members to be more alert to their own life changes, and for managers to be more alert to the differing vulnerability of individuals during periods of organisation alignment. The culture of an organisation and management styles are major factors during such transitions. High control culture organisations and a directive style will tend to inhibit the transformation required, whereas a consultative and supportive approach and culture are more likely to lead to the successful implementation of the move to virtual team working. Managers need to be skilled leaders, coaches and guides.

Consider the following situation: a manager in a global oilfield business agreed to submit a bid for the installation of oilfield technology equipment in the field for a major client. The delivery of the bid required expertise from research centres and business units in a range of geographical areas. With a short time-line, limited resources and the daily demands on key staff in the field, the bid manager was confronted with organising and delivering a viable bid.

What would you have done? In theory, in such a situation, many organisations would have organised a virtual team consisting of a series of experts and staff to contribute to the development of the bid via the use of technology. Some organisations even have in place a set of processes and structures to ensure the timely delivery of a bid to include a 'stage and gate' development system and bid review sessions.

What actually happened? Managers reported that these systems are used in principle but not in practice. In fact a small number of people worked overtime, often doing special deals, calling in favours or using influence to get things done. These systems are called espoused 'as if' systems, which managers use in theory as a management tool but which are neither viable nor do-able in practice.

To maximise the effectiveness of your virtual teams will require you to adapt and adjust and fine-tune. Inflexible policies and procedures do not provide sufficient support for collaboration between virtual team members, who are expected to grapple with uncertainty, innovate, and remain flexible. It is critical for your organisation to be able to establish and monitor the balance between changing needs if virtual team working is to prove successful in the longer term.

Decision-making supports alignment. On virtual teams, the leader's role in fostering alignment leads, in large part, to consistency and predictability in the team's decision-making. Each team member brings, during the life of a virtual team, their personal decision-making style. Indeed, the virtual team will adopt a dominant decision-making style that becomes embedded in the culture of the team.

"Change is not a destination, just as hope is not a strategy."

Rudy Giuliani

How do you enhance communication in team decision-making?

Figure 11 Tips for communicating with different decision-making styles

DECISIVE	HIERARCHIC
Be on time	Be prepared; do your homework
Minimise chit-chat	Get and use their input
Get to the point	Present information and conclusions clearly
Be self-assured and positive	Show your reasoning and logic
Make clear recommendations	Expect proposals to be 'corrected'
Stress bottom line benefits	Listen well
Avoid too much detail	Do not press for quick agreement
Answer questions directly	Allow time to mull things over
	Be willing to share credit

FLEXIBLE	INTEGRATIVE
Keep things informal	Share information from varied sources
Keep an open mind about solutions	Solicit their ideas and information
Be willing to shift topics	Invite people to participate in problem solving and idea generation
Stress options and choices	Communicate hunches
Don't push for long term commitment	Explore positives and negatives of proposed solutions
Keep conversation moving	Be willing to modify your ideas
	Avoid absolutes
	Do not press for quick decisions

Source: *The Dynamic Decision Maker*, Michael Driver & Kenneth Brousseau

To foster alignment in decision-making, considering the following questions improves the decision-making readiness of virtual team.

1. Is a solution absolutely critical?

2. Do we have enough information to make a good decision?

3. Is the problem or issue structured so that it is clearly defined, organised and has recognised solutions?

4. Do the members of the virtual team have to agree and accept a decision for it to work?

5. Are virtual team members aligned with the same goals that you are trying to achieve?

6. Is disagreement likely among virtual teams members in reaching a decision?

Alignment does not guarantee high performing virtual teams – it is one ingredient in the mix of high performing virtual teams.

How do we implement alignment?

At the inception of virtual teams, you are encouraged to agree protocols for the following:

- defining the team's 'magnetic north' for its work; this supports the vision and strategy
- the information virtual team members need to know
- the frequency and style of communication to manage ambiguity and flexibility of working
- the tools to manage conflicts, take decisions and deliver information to key stakeholders
- the changes and modifications in the performance management system required to support virtual team-based working
- the actions needed to be taken as a leader and member of a virtual team to thrive on the Transition Curve.

QUESTIONS FOR YOU TO CONSIDER

1. How adaptable is your management in supporting your virtual team's actions to achieve alignment?

2. Is your management ready to accept possible lack of control and the ambiguity that is fostered when employees work as a virtual team?

3. Does your performance management system enable virtual team assessments as well as individual assessments?

4. How is virtual team performance rewarded in your organisation?

THE WIS STORY – PART SEVEN

The strategic importance of the KSI project together with the global nature of the virtual team provided major challenges to implementing new ways of working. It was not an easy transition. Once the vision was clear, the team manager and members of the team took time to consider how well the organisational systems, structures and processes were adapted to virtual team working – were they fit for purpose ? Discussions were held with senior management to negotiate more flexibility. Anxiety and resistance was manifest in some individuals. Some expressed concern that as virtual workers they might become overlooked for development opportunities and promotions. Others were anxious about becoming a member of a virtual team as they did not understand how their performance would be assessed by a manager or team leader they did not see every day.

One key change was to review and revise the performance review process. This enabled both team and individual performance to be recognised. Appraisals were carried out using the new balanced score card performance review process, with the team manager assessing the team performance of virtual team members, and line managers assessing their individual performance. Integral to each individual's development plan, was the opportunity to get involved in training events and networking face-to-face. This was a great motivator as they felt they were being recognised and not forgotten. Support through the organisation's mentoring and coaching schemes was taken up by many, who were finding the transition process turbulent and painful.

case study the WIS story

chapter 9

let's go!

developing virtual team excellence in your organisation

*"We are what we repeatedly do.
Excellence, therefore, is not an act, but a habit."*

Aristotle

I n the previous chapters we examined the core factors that inform the Virtual Team Model (VTM). For your convenience we provide a summary below, followed by a number of tools and techniques, which you may find useful in promoting, developing and launching virtual team working to ensure your organisation makes the most of modern ways of working.

Effective orientation: this provides a realistic review and outlook within the organisation for the support and role of virtual teams. It includes a relevant and compelling narrative, clarifying the value of the work to the larger business, and a clear definition of team member contributions and participation, inclusive of expectations of individuals and the team as a whole.

Participative or collaborative planning as a team: an organisation may provide virtual team members with a document to 'communicate' the vision and goals of the project. This will enable the team to define their roles, rules for working and manner and scope of communication and technology, and provide them with the opportunity to take decisions on how to achieve their goals. The key criterion here is that the team takes the lead on these activities with the support of management.

Effective communication: it is essential to clearly define the tools for communicating whilst appreciating the common communication barriers that exist in human and technology-based communication.

Relationship building: it is important to recognise the emotional as well as cultural dimensions essential for developing the necessary discipline to work as a virtual team.

Building of trust: this is an essential ingredient for success, particularly when virtual team members are dispersed across time zones and long distances. Consistency in words and actions, along with bringing to the surface those issues that keep them from working effectively, are critical success factors.

Performance management: managers, team leaders and virtual team members need to set clear, detailed and task-specific performance goals. Productive virtual team members thrive on both themselves and their managers giving feedback formally and informally in culturally appropriate ways. Furthermore the organisation performance management system will need to be outcome focused, and take into account the unique features of virtual team working.

Mentoring and career management: members are often selected for virtual teams by managers without consideration of the impact on career development and the level of competencies to deliver results. Such individuals may become isolated from performance reviews or have

Virtual Team Model (VTM)

© Shawn Ireland 2012

managers unable to assess performance due to lack of oversight or contact with the work of virtual team members. Team members should keep records of their achievements.

Cultural fluency: the work of many virtual teams is compromised by the failure of team members to consider the impact of national and regional cultures. Cultural differences are not just based on nationality but on a unique set of behavioural, language and relationship variables.

Stakeholder management: virtual team members identify key stakeholders and their positions towards the work of the team. This involves defining the sources of power, which make things happen, and who will have the most impact on the work of the team. Developing a stakeholder strategy provides agreed actions to influence the impact of stakeholders in the team achieving their goals.

Use of technology: an assessment of the limits and opportunities of the organisation's technology assets to assist the work of the virtual team is crucial.

Networking: it is important to understand and manage the systems and structures in the organisation in the service of virtual team working.

Managing the paradox of structure and adaptability: productive virtual teams will need some level of structure. This requires negotiations with management to enable the teams to develop their own structures, possibly outside the scope of standard organisation practice, to support their work.

With this in mind, we offer the following guidelines to prepare your organisation for the transition to virtual team work:

1. Create and communicate a 'shared' vision and expectations

In simple, direct terms describe your vision for virtual team work and create time to discuss and clarify the expectations of other team members for working virtually. Taking the time to discuss expectations offers an opportunity for members and leaders to address resistance and anxiety. This is especially relevant if team members have previous virtual team experience to draw on in these discussions.

Do not underestimate the value of these discussions before and during the life of a virtual team. They can take place using any form of technology that allows maximum flexibility and interaction.

2. Prepare and directly address the past practices and new opportunities

One of the common refrains heard when initiating virtual team work is *"will they ever learn from the past?"* Whilst most organisations experience positive performance and business results using virtual teams, the approach is not always embraced nor positive in some instances. If your organisation has had diverse experience with virtual team work, address the issues directly. You may be familiar with the idiom *the elephant in the room* referring to obvious problems or issues no-one wants to discuss. Address the failures, difficult issues and learning from any post-mortems. This establishes the culture of openness and transparency that is essential for virtual team success.

3. Generate a sense of urgency

Urgency not panic. The shift to working virtually will foster resistance and discomfort. Urgency indicates importance of team goals and seriousness of intent. We noted earlier that distance and lack of consistent contact and human interface generate discomfort and lack of focus for many members. We often hear comments *"I thought I had been forgotten"* or *"it feels like I am working in a vacuum"* or even *"time seems to slow down on virtual teams."* Urgency fosters attention, focus and intention – key ingredients for virtual team performance.

4. Identify influencers and work to develop a leadership coalition to guide the transition

Surprisingly there is frequently a lack of stakeholder analysis and management on virtual project teams and work teams. The fluid nature and situational demands of internal and external stakeholders requires vigilance on the part of team members. Virtual working requires a consistent review of stakeholder requirements, their power and position on issues and a coordinated strategy for actions when interacting with stakeholders. Remember, distance requires consistent interactions and coordinated strategies for interacting with stakeholders. The lack of a clearly defined stakeholder management plan breeds inconsistency, lack of coordination and communication vacuums which, if our experience is any indicator, is often filled with information not helpful to the team.

5. Anticipate and line up political sponsorship

Consistent with stakeholder action planning, this is offering a brutally honest assessment of the political environment within and outside the organisation that may impact the work of the team and its vision and strategy. Assessing who has the power, including control and influence, and who simply reacts to you and your stakeholders, is a critical part of the initial and on-going work of the team. Whilst we recommend flexibility when reviewing your stakeholder management plan, we recommend weekly or monthly reviews depending on the nature and scope of the virtual team's work.

6. Deliberately draft an implementation plan to achieve noticeable, verifiable small, short term 'wins'

Depending on your team's experience working virtually, identify opportunities to achieve and celebrate success working as a virtual team. They can be simple or complex in nature. The goal is to send a message to the team and immediate stakeholders that the team is functioning well virtually. Examples may include agreement on steps for a project plan, a successful *Webex* or *Skype* meeting, delivery of a first draft of a report. Simple and small 'wins' in the beginning phases of a team's life are critical.

7. Identify systems and structures that are virtual team friendly in the organisation

We noted earlier that virtual teams often challenge the formal systems and structures for getting the work done in your organisation. Indeed, many systems (technology, performance, assessment) are designed with intact or co-located staff in mind. Many organisations view work in a mechanistic manner developing these systems to provide consistency, control and predictability. Working in a virtual team requires modifying and often revising systems to meet the remote nature of working. Identifying those systems and work requirements that keep the team from working effectively is critical.

For example, organisation performance management systems are often designed to support individual rather than team performance.

Discuss with stakeholders any flexibility in reconfiguring key performance indicators (KPIs) to gain team-based performance outcomes and measures.

8. Keep key managers and leaders informed on a regular basis of your progress and challenge

The outcome of a mechanistic view of human behaviour is the assumption made by many managers that if an employee is not seen working, they may not be working with the same level of commitment and intent than when directly observed. This is especially true in situations of high resource demand or crisis situations.

Intentionally and consistently interacting with your direct managers and leaders on your team's progress, offers strategic and political reciprocity when support may be required at a later date, keeps the work of the team in perspective, and allows you to shape the narrative in the organisation on the work of your team. We recommend erring on the side of initially over-communicating until the team has firmly engaged in the Invest stage of development.

9. Plan for resistance, support intentionality in addressing conflicts that arise

This builds trust-based relationships. We stressed earlier the need to be intentional in addressing the issues that arise when organising and working as a virtual team. Expect and plan for the expression of conflicts on your team. This requires being mindful of the challenges faced by members in delivering, being transparent in addressing conflict and seeking solutions agreed by the team. This takes time but taking the time up front will save time later on.

10. Review, revise and re-do to enshrine new behaviours

Virtual teams do not operate in a static, predictable environment. Set aside reflection time weekly to document the issues and deliverables of your team. Identify two items to revisit the following day or week and action steps you are considering. Place them in a diary or notebook and revisit the following week. Revise and update weekly. This will offer a journal of your journey as a virtual team leader.

THE WIS STORY – PART EIGHT

The .planning phase took several months, to ensure the organisation and the virtual team were ready for the big push to launch the KSI project.

Having gained senior management support for virtual team working on the KSI project, the project sponsor had worked hard to explain the nature and importance of the project and how it fitted with the organisation's vision and strategy, and promote the value of the KSI virtual team to the wider organisation globally. Members of the team had been selected from across the organisation and after the initial face-to-face meeting participated as a team in the planning. They defined and agreed the project goals, the technologies to communicate and share information, and the role and responsibilities of each team member. They carried out a stakeholder analysis to assess where the greatest impact on their work would come from, and agreed a stakeholder strategy so that stakeholders would have a positive effect on them reaching their goal.

Building a trust relationship between virtual team members was crucial for success. In addition to the face-to-face meetings and team building activities, the training sessions on cross-cultural communication and critical thinking provided great opportunities for team members to understand and get to know each other and their capabilities better.

Performance management and career management anxieties expressed by team members were addressed, and coaching and mentoring opportunities made available to them. These provided some reassurance and structure to individuals, who were concerned that they might be overlooked for promotions while working on the virtual project team.

continued opposite

case study the WIS story

THE WIS STORY – PART EIGHT   *continued*

They would be working in a challenging environment, so transitioning rapidly to feeling they could thrive on the project, was key.

Everything was in place to launch the KSI project, although the team manager and team members recognised that the road ahead could develop any number of potholes, so actions would need to be reviewed on a regular basis.

To launch the KSI project, the chief executive of WIS recorded a short video explaining the strategic importance of the project to the whole organisation, and seeking the cooperation of all employees. The virtual team members were introduced to the organisation. This video was made available online to all the businesses worldwide, so that local employees could view it at local time.

And what happened? The KSI project was delivered on time and on budget. In fact, the post-mortem data was used to inform the setting up of other virtual teams. The organisation also decided to build on the experiences of the virtual team members on the project, to develop a best practice computer-based simulation. This action-learning tool was made available via an intranet to all regions to support the further development of global virtual team working.

case study

the WIS story

Now let us take a step-by-step approach to developing and promoting virtual teams in your organisation.

Start by considering the differences between management practice in your organisation and the practices of virtual teams.

Figure 12 Business management practices versus virtual team practices

BUSINESS MANAGEMENT PRACTICES	VIRTUAL TEAM PRACTICES
Work with systems and processes already known	Link goals to the organisation strategies
Have many objectives and goals	Leverage technology to work with unknown systems and processes
Use people locally with similar values and experiences	Draw on and develop talent across the organisation world-wide
Provide greater certainty and less risks (outcomes, cost)	Involve individuals with different values, experiences and skills
Support the status quo	Are temporary in composition based on business need
	May represent higher risks (outcomes, time-lines)
	Disturb the status quo

Then you will need to consider the skills managers and virtual team leaders have or need to develop to manage such teams effectively. (see Figure 13, Skills to manage virtual teams effectively opposite).

You will need to diagnose the potential challenges of virtual teams in your organisation. Figure 14, Challenges of virtual teams (on page 104) may be of help when you start reflecting on the process.

Figure 13 Skills to manage virtual teams effectively

INTERPERSONAL SKILLS	Ability to build rapport and relationships quickly and then sustain them Precision questioning Excellent listener – spots underlying meanings and process messages Tests out meaning by summarising and reflecting Trusts intuition Understands and pays attention to cultural difference Motivates remotely Gets things done through influence rather than authority
USE OF MEDIA	Clear, direct and concise Flexible in uses of different media Matches message to personal preference Doesn't swamp people with data Includes social content in electronic messages
OUTCOMES ORIENTED	Establishes clear accountabilities Establishes clear measures and standards of performance Focuses on outcomes and deliverables rather than activities Sets up agreed monitoring arrangements Maintains focus on both immediate urgent and long-term goals
MODELLING A HIGH TRUST RELATIONSHIP	Gives lots of rope Able to operate away from a command and control leadership style Sticks by word and commitments Macro rather than micro manages Demonstrates confidence in others
FOSTERING A COLLABORATIVE CULTURE	Assesses suitability for remote working Makes people feel part of a team Makes themselves available to coach and counsel Provides clarity over team member roles and interdependencies Committed to making time for team development Responds quickly and supportively to crises
STANDING BACK FROM THE ACTION	Links what people do to the wider organisation Networks extensively with customers and suppliers Able to picture position on the ground Manages time to maintain and schedule social contact

Adapted from: A Smith & A Sinclair, Roffey Park, 2003

Figure 14 Challenges of virtual teams

Based on your experience or opinion, what problems are more likely to occur with virtual teams and remote workers than with those that are co-located?

_____

_____

_____

_____

_____

What is easier about leading a team that is virtual?

_____

_____

_____

_____

_____

What is more difficult about leading a team that is virtual?

_____

_____

_____

_____

_____

Next, you will need to define the roles fulfilled by virtual team members. These are varied and may be categorised into two areas: coordination and collaboration roles, and autonomy roles, as set out in Figure 15.

Figure 15 Virtual team member roles

COORDINATION AND COLLABORATION ROLES	AUTONOMY ROLES
Keep local managers and stakeholders informed of your work	Act as self managing team members by assuming accountability and leadership in their areas of expertise and by delivering quality services/products on time
Keep team members informed of the concerns, interests and reactions of their functional areas, local stakeholders and management	Take responsibility for identifying and reconciling team and local needs as well as priorities of other teams on which team members serve
Coordinate and communicate with other team members to ensure that all are aware of who is performing what activities, and that everyone has access to important documents and other information	Clarify ambiguous tasks with the team leader and with other team members
Build and maintain trust with other virtual team members by demonstrating reliable performance, integrity and concern for others	Address conflicting loyalties
Share learning from their experiences with other team members and with their local organisations	

Adapted from: Deborah Duarte & Nancy Snyder

Selecting employees for virtual teams is not necessarily straightforward. Not everyone will feel comfortable working in a virtual team, preferring the social interaction of being co-located with their colleagues. Some may not possess the required motivation, commitment and skills, and may be overwhelmed by the technology involved. Figure 16 provides some common criteria for you to consider when selecting employees for virtual teams.

Figure 16 Selecting employees for virtual teams

COMMON SELECTION CRITERIA

Technical and functional skill or skill potential

Problem solving skills

Interpersonal skills

Enthusiasm for the project

Time to participate in the project

Willingness to participate in the project

Lack of conflicts that will interfere with the project

A high degree of self-motivation

Ability and opportunity to work with communication and collaboration software

An understanding of project management tools and techniques

Once virtual team members have been selected, you will find it very useful to ask each of them to complete the assessment on pages 107 & 108 (Figure 17, Virtual team working readiness assessment), to find out whether they are really ready for virtual team working. If you identify any gaps, appropriate actions can be taken prior to the team starting work virtually, for example training on skills gaps, or removal from the virtual team and selection of another individual.

Figure 17 Virtual team working readiness assessment

Rate the extent to which you agree with each statement, using the following scale:

| 1 strongly disagree | 2 disagree | 3 neutral | 4 agree | 5 strongly agree |

	1	2	3	4	5
ATTRACT AND ALIGN					
1. The purpose of working virtually as a team is clear to me					
2. The benefits and threats of working virtually have been discussed/agreed					
3. The team has the basic skills necessary to be a success working in a virtual setting					
4. Everyone on the team shares the same purpose					
5. The team is about the right size					
BUILD PRODUCTIVE RELATIONSHIPS					
6. A basic level of trust is present among members to work effectively with each other					
7. I can rely on my colleagues in the team to do what they say they will do					
8. Our team has about the right level of diversity it needs to be effective					
9. We value a range of styles and types of people and behaviour in the team					
10. Reporting structures and relationships in the team are clear to me					
11. I feel I have the authority I need to get my job done within the team					
AGREE DEPENDENCIES					
12. My personal goals and performance objectives as a member of the team are clear to me					
13. I know and understand the goals and objectives of others in the team					
14. We have about the right balance of control and autonomy in the team					
15. I can count on the cooperation of the others in the team to meet my/our objectives					
16. We usually meet our objectives					
17. The objectives of team members do not conflict in a significant way with each other					

continued overleaf

VIRTUAL TEAM WORKING READINESS ASSESSMENT *(continued from previous page)*

1 strongly disagree	2 disagree	3 neutral	4 agree	5 strongly agree

	1	2	3	4	5

MANAGE YOURSELF/ADD VALUE TO OTHERS

		1	2	3	4	5
18.	The amount of travel we have to do is ok					
19.	I see other team members as often as I need to					
20.	I see my manager as often as I need to					
21.	I think the activities of the team are visible to the organisation					
22.	I am clear about the expectations other members of the team have of me					
23.	I get about the right level of performance feedback from my manager					

IMPROVE CONNECTIONS

		1	2	3	4	5
24.	We communicate well in the team and work (or will work) well virtually					
25.	We use the available communication technologies effectively in the team					
26.	Language and culture are not barriers to communication in the team					
27.	The members of the team have the right level of communication skills					
28.	We work together well as a team					

FACILITATE LEARNING

		1	2	3	4	5
29.	Members of the team learn effectively from one another					
30.	The team is good at continuously improving its performance					
31.	We regularly review the process of how we work and the content of what we do					
32.	The team has good contacts with the rest of the organisation					
33.	Team members are generally receptive to outside ideas and new initiatives					

Launching virtual teams

When you are ready to start virtual team working, there are a number of things you need to undertake to ensure a successful launch. These are listed in Figure 18.

Figure 18 Launching virtual teams

INITIATING COMMUNICATION WITH THE TEAM	ORIENTING INDIVIDUALS AND THE TEAM
Call or visit each individual personally	Schedule a face-to-face meeting with all team members
Provide a mechanism by which team members can learn about each other	Orient individuals and the team to the goals
Send all team members information about the team	Develop virtual team working norms
Answer individuals' questions about the work	Develop a technology plan
Determine whether or not individuals have any hardware or software compatibility or use issues	Develop a communication plan
	Facilitate team building

Adapted from: Deborah Duarte & Nancy Snyder

Once you have launched the virtual team, you will need to continue to develop team members and keep them on track.

Inevitably, problems will arise from time to time with virtual teams. You will need to address these promptly to ensure they do not have a negative impact on individuals and the team achieving their goals effectively. In Figure 19, Common virtual team problems (overleaf) are some of the most common issues that you may encounter.

Figure 19 Common virtual team problems

SYMPTOMS	POSSIBLE CAUSES/INTERVENTIONS
The team cannot get beyond the early stages of team building	Symptomatic of underlying issues. Review the team's composition and charter. The inception phase requires creativity and less control. As the manager are you modelling these attributes?
The team appears to be stuck and is not moving towards execution	Assess the team in terms of task and social dynamics, and environmental factors. Go back and review expectations and identify obstacles to meeting those expectations.
A few team members seem to be doing all of the work	Talk (voice-to-voice) to all members separately to determine the reason(s) for the differences in contributions. Are tasks allocated properly? Are some team members clustered in one geography or culture? Is communication streamlined and straightforward?
Team members do not appear to be applying sufficient effort to the team's task	Talk (voice-to-voice) with those who are disengaged to determine the reason for effort and performance that is not congruent with team standards. Are the expectations unrealistic? Do they lack information / skills / training to be successful? Do they need a mentor? Are the non-performers in a matrix, rather than a linear, relationship? Are there conflicting objectives?
The team misses or almost misses a deadline to deliverables	Determine root cause and take corrective action. Employ a deeper level of project management skills or assign a trained project manager to the team.
Conflict arises that derails the team's progress	Is the cause of the conflict task related or social/cultural in nature? Take action that is appropriate to the cultural and/or social issue.
Team members who are not co-located seem to be fading into obscurity	Work with the team leader to keep a record of contact with team members. Encourage team leaders to spend 70-80% of their time (virtual or face-to-face) with team members who are not co-located.

Planning for virtual team success

The success of virtual teams does not just happen. Typically, a champion or someone dedicated to making something happen through intuition, force of personality, planning, or just plain luck, makes the team. But given the potential for team payback, can we afford to leave virtual team development to intuition or luck?

Several characteristics seem to distinguish more successful from less successful virtual teams – the 'good' ones have them and the 'not so good' don't. By analysing these factors a better plan for good individual and team performance emerges. See Figure 20.

Figure 20 Characteristics of successful virtual teams

A dedicated champion 'owns' and starts the process

Established urgency and boundaries

Members selected for skill potential not personality, status or 'fit'

An architecture is established for early meeting process

Clear rules of behaviour are set

The team selects and seizes critical few tasks, goals and measures

Assumptions are challenged with facts and new information

Time is spent together

Feedback, recognition, and rewards are exploited

By taking time to follow these steps you will ensure the successful and effective implementation of virtual teams in your organisation, and achieve Virtual Team Excellence.

"Whatever you can do, or dream you can, begin it.
Boldness has genius, magic, and power in it."

Goethe

chapter 10

... and beyond

"The organisations that will truly excel in the future will be the organisations that discover how to tap people's commitment and capacity to learn at ALL levels in an organisation."

Peter Senge, The Fifth Discipline

Where do we go from here?

From a leadership point of view, it has never been easier to work closely with colleagues in distant locations or to hold meetings with other members of the team around the globe. In practical terms many hurdles remain – hurdles which organisations cannot ignore if they want to utilise their global talent effectively. We have more options and choices at our disposal to deliver business results using virtual teams.

We suggest the increasing use of virtual teams requires attention to communication, relationships, technology and culture requirements. We have identified seven organisational core competencies critical to virtual team excellence and success, as demonstrated in the Virtual Team Model – vision, involvement, relationships, technology, understanding, alignment, and launching successfully. Virtual team working/teleworking are increasingly becoming a key feature in today's organisations. In the USA, it has been calculated that if the 40% of employees who could work from home did so for half the week, the country could, *'reduce road travel by 91 billion miles/year, reduce greenhouse gases by 51 million tons/year, and save 281 million barrels of oil a year* (Source: *Telework Research Network* (2010), *Workshifting Benefits: the Bottom Line*). The size, nature of the business culture, competitive environment and strategic business goals will define the value given to a virtual team work environment.

From a technology point of view, technology developments will no doubt make virtual team working even easier, faster and more efficient. Already *WiFi*, the *Cloud* and *4G* systems for ultra-broadband internet access mean communication contact has become easier – any time, any place. Yet not all organisations embrace the technological requirements of virtual team work as a viable extension of the workplace or see the value in leveraging technology. *Yahoo!* was one of the first large organisations to announce it was banning working from home to improve communication and team collaboration so that employees become more engaged and productive. This appears to be a strategic business decision to realign the culture of the organisation to meet competitive market pressures and regain its place in the technology market.

From a business point of view, the key issue is the value proposition of virtual team work. At the beginning of this book we posed the following questions: *'What is the value proposition of virtual teamwork? Why should an organisation use virtual team work to deliver value or better solve a problem than other forms of working?'* Virtual team work is one tool in a business arsenal for meeting the needs of customers and stakeholders. It is not a panacea to business success, nor does it guarantee business success. The Virtual Team Model provides a roadmap to develop these assets in the service of creating value for working in a virtual team environment.

We maintain that to create value is to foster a sustainable, high performing virtual team culture. The sustainability of each virtual team core competency requires a commitment to challenge complacency, test the limits of tolerance for ambiguity and question the assumptions inherent in the business strategy. In our experience, the key to sustainability is to link directly individual employee development with the development of the virtual team core competencies. A useful model to develop this link is the Performance Development Model (PDM) outlined in Figure 21. The PDM links ongoing development needs of individuals with the strategic needs of the business. Through the use of virtual teams and action-based learning, it optimises an organisation's capability to leverage the potential of employees in different countries, regions, and cities, in the service of the strategic goals of the business.

Figure 21 Performance Development Model (PDM)

© Shawn Ireland

The Organisational Core Competency Agenda (OCCA) comprises the competencies framework developed from an audit of the skills requirements of an organisation, and the development needs of individuals ascertained through, for example, the performance review process. With this information in mind, you can launch projects globally using virtual team members, who will be supported by internal expertise in the particular project topic area, and by the stakeholders who have a vested interest in the successful delivery of the project. The PDM approach links the on-going development needs of individuals and virtual teams with measurable outcomes that meet the strategic requirements of the customer and the organisation. It also optimises the organisation's capability to transform human potential in the service of the strategic business goals, through the use of action-based learning.

With the increased emphasis on developing management tools that better leverage the assets of an organisation, managers and leaders are more and more focused on the use of virtual teams. Leading thinkers and decision-makers have been attempting to identify what a high performing organisation may look like in the future. The one common theme emerging provides a picture of a simpler, more flexible organisation, less focused on command and control systems, and more geared to delegating responsibility based on trust to their teams. The success of virtual teams, however, rests on management and key decision-makers understanding that to support productive virtual teams requires these performance development elements today, not tomorrow.

"In the current economic environment it's vital that businesses make the most of opportunities to save money while improving business performance. The desk-bound, building-based work model no longer works for every business."

Jeroen Hoencamp, CEO, Vodafone UK

From a competitive and strategic point of view, the business environment places a premium on the quality and speed of solutions. Agility and flexibility in delivering products and services, responsiveness to customer and market-place demands and an engaged workforce are the holy grail of successful businesses. We argue that virtual team work is one of the strategic tools to capture the human potential of a business to get ahead and keep ahead of the curve. To do so requires managers to be clear and focused in the communication of the business strategy.

In our practice, we often ask managers to articulate the key strategic goals of their organisation. With a few exceptions, we confront moments of silence or hesitation as managers consider the question and struggle to share the strategy. The language of many strategic statements is inaccessible, irrelevant to, or inconsistent with, employees' and team members' daily work experiences. This is especially noticeable in a virtual working environment.

Herein lies your challenge as a manager of virtual teams – to translate the key strategic goals of the business into language that is easy to understand, relevant and meaningful to members of the virtual team. This is one of the core animating principles behind the success of virtual team work – making the business strategy come alive for team members. Consistently review and debate the terms of the team's work against the strategy of the business. Seek clarity to the following questions:

1. What must be created?

2. What must stop?

3. With whom do I interact to sustain the work of the team?

The answers to these questions engage members and provide an opportunity to critique and review performance against expectations.

What does the future hold?

Advances in technology are offering new and exciting tools for enhancing the value of virtual team work. We are working on business simulation technology that will enable virtual team members to develop core competencies using real-time avatars and coaches from multiple sites locally or globally. Development sessions can occur real-time, anywhere in the world and foster opportunities to test ideas, competencies and innovative strategies in a simulated business environment.

Advances in modelling technology will enable team members to predict future trends and experience virtually the outcomes. An oilfield company using virtual teams is now able to enter an oil molecule, walk around and explore its core elements, test how their actions impact the molecule and assess outcomes. The same technology is being developed for use by surgical teams as they address critical decisions in a medical setting. These are exciting advancements and enable virtual teams to be more focused and innovative in their work. Yet, these are only tools.

The sustainable success of virtual team work rests with harnessing the human potential of its members. By understanding the challenges and opportunities of working in virtual teams and managing virtual staff, you, as leaders and managers and virtual team members, will all be better prepared and able to take advantage of the strengths of virtual team working to promote success and ultimately achieve Virtual Team Excellence.

further information

To find out more about Virtual Team Excellence workshops or to order additional copies of the book, contact HRCgroup via email at info@hrc-group.com or visit our website at www.hrc-group.com

References

The Amplified Enterprise: Using Social Media To Expand Organizational Capabilities
Bradley, A & McDonald, M (November 2011),
Big Idea: Social Business Interview (interviewer David Kiron)

The Challenge Of The Virtual Team
Clutterbuck, D (2004). Training Journal

Culture and Organizations: A Software of the Mind
Hofstede, G (1991), London, McGraw-Hill Publishers

Drive: The Surprising Truth about What Motivates Us
Pink, D (2010), Canongate Books

Facilitating Work Team Effectiveness
Buzaglo, G & Wheelan, S (February 1999) Small Group Research, Sage Publication

Future Work: How Businesses Can Adapt And Thrive In The New World Of Work
Maitland, A & Thomson, P (2011), Palgrave MacMillan

IFRAME: A Manager's Guide to Critically Balanced Thinking
Kelton, L & Ireland, S (2009), British Columbia, Murray Creative Info Solutions

Managing a Virtual Workplace
Cascio, Wayne F (2001), Academy of Management Executives

Mastering Virtual Teams: Strategies, Tools and Techniques that Succeed
Durante, D & Snyder, N (2001), San Francisco, Jossey-Bass

People Management: Challenges and Opportunities. Cultural Fluency
Rees, D (2002), Palgrave Macmillan

The Power Of Habit – Why We Do What We Do And How To Change
Duhigg, C (2012), Random House

Remote and Virtual Working: Friend or Foe?
Mulkeen, D (2007), Training Journal

Virtual Teams: People Working across Boundaries and Technology
Lipnack, J & Stamps, J (2000), John Wiley & Sons

Virtual Teams that Work: Creating Conditions for Effective Virtual Teams
Cohen, S & Gibson, C (2003), San Francisco, Jossey-Bass

What Makes an Excellent Virtual Manager
Smith, A & Sinclair, A (2003), Roffey Park

about the authors

Shawn Ireland, PhD, MSc, is Managing Director of HRCgroup, a global learning and organisational development practice based in London, UK, Singapore and Vancouver, Canada. Shawn has been practising as a business psychologist for over 30 years, working with private, public and third sector organisations worldwide to improve leadership and critical thinking, manage individual and organisational performance, initiate change, and consult on the effective use of virtual teams and remote working.

Paula Hart, BSc (Hons), is an associate and coach with HRCgroup. Paula has more than 25 years' experience in the learning and development environment with international and small and medium sized organisations. Her areas of expertise include: cross-cultural understanding and communication; virtual team working; leadership development; and coaching/mentoring. She is bilingual in French and English.